The Caregiver's Secrets

By Willetha King Barnette
with Harold Barnette

Published by
Institute for Family Caregiving, Inc.

ISBN 978-0-9982032-2-5
EBook ISBN 978-0-9982032-0-1

1. Caregiving—aging—elder care—United States 2. Medical services—geriatrics—patient advocacy—United States 3. Coordination of care—assisted living—care planning—United States.

This book represents the author's experience as a family caregiver and is not intended to convey legal, financial, or medical advice. Persons in need of such advice should seek appropriate professional consultation.

Printed in the United States of America
First printing December 2016

Dedication

For *A. Ruth Jackson King*
and *Joyce Naiomi Barnette*

Table of Contents

SEVEN PRINCIPLES OF CAREGIVING

Help without hurting. Be willing, able, and knowledgeable of your responsibilities.

Be legal. Have the formal authority to represent and make decisions for the person in your care.

Accept assistance. Do not attempt to go it alone.

Avoid panic. Be a calm presence. Offer measured responses.

Be a "healing team" player: patient/caregiver/ family/professional providers/community.

Safety first. Adopt best practices and avoid unnecessary risks.

Seek respite and be vigilant about self-care.

INTRODUCTION

A storm is coming. And most of us are not ready for it. It will be a storm of older people. Mothers, fathers, siblings, aunts, uncles, friends, neighbors. The leading edge of that storm has arrived. Over the next twenty or so years one out of every five people in our society will be more than sixty-five years old. I know because as a baby boomer I will be one of them. Many of my generation will live well into their eighties and nineties. Our society has never before had to deal with so many elderly people. So we have not prepared. We are not ready.

But this book isn't about my generation or me. It is mostly about my mother, for whom I served as caregiver for over twenty years. When my mother came to live with me in 1989 I had no idea we would share a household for almost twenty-five years, until she was deep into her eighties and I was forced to place her into a personal care facility. Mom went from being a cheerful, bright, fiercely independent sixty-five year old to being frail and forgetful, reduced to a mere fragment of her former self. And it all occurred so gradually that when I finally realized the extent of her decline it came as a surprise.

At that time I was thirty-six, the single mom of a bright middle school daughter and working two jobs—a full-time position at a local university that paid the main bills, and a part-time job that afforded us some financial wiggle room and a few special treats. I also had health issues. A decade before I had been diagnosed with Crohn's disease, an incurable inflammatory bowel disease that had to be treated with increasingly powerful and expensive medications. So Mom's arrival was in many ways a godsend. She was there when my latchkey daughter got home from school. A great cook; she shared duties in the kitchen, and helped with housework. When my illness flared up I could rely on her for help. She even picked up temporary part-time job assignments here and there to supplement her small pension and was good about helping with household bills. All in all having Mom in the household was a good deal for everyone.

I had always felt close to my mother. As a middle child with an older brother and sister and a younger brother, the years separating my birth from my siblings were significant in childhood. I was too young to mingle and play with my older siblings and their friends, so even before my younger brother came along, I spent a lot of time alone with Mom. My older brother and sister were in school during most days and my dad, a school principal, worked long hours at his job. So it was just the two of us doing things around the house, me watching and helping her in the kitchen, going shopping, and doing girly stuff. We got to know each other really well. We enjoyed each other. That fondness carried over into adulthood.

So when Mom began her decline it wasn't just a sense of losing a parent, but of witnessing the gradual fading away of a close friend. I wasn't prepared. Looking back over the span of years, everything seems so clear. But in the blur of everyday life, it was easy to miss the early warning signs. Mom would forget to do important things, like take her medicine. I would come home to the smell of burned food, or find ruined meals or pots discarded in the trash. During our first few years together Mom had a big old land yacht of a car, a clunker that she somehow kept running. She regularly made the two-hour drive to visit friends in our little hometown and was active in church and volunteer activities. But then she began to have accidents, mostly fender benders. There was evidence of her getting disoriented or lost, such as making a supposedly quick shopping trip and being gone for hours. So she stopped driving. She had to. Multiple hip replacement surgeries and a series of other health issues including high blood pressure and congestive heart disease began to take their toll. But I was in the day-to-day mode of solving problems as they occurred, so I did not grasp the big picture. I didn't have the presence of mind to step back and add it all up.

I assumed more and more responsibility for my mother's affairs even though it was enough of a challenge to manage the logistics and finances of my own life. Taking on my mom's responsibilities presented a whole new set of demands for which I was totally unprepared. The scope and range of things that I had to deal with shifted dramatically. Suddenly I was managing her doctor's appointments and making sure her meds were taken on schedule. I was dealing with emergency rooms, urgent care clinics, hospitals, and third party payment bureaucracies such as Medicare and the Veterans Administration. I was buying equipment to help her complete her personal care independently. And eventually I was buying adult diapers in a daily battle with incontinence. A 25-year sojourn started with my mom as a fit and active 65-year-old, and ended in stages, with her residency in a nursing home, changed by congestive heart failure, vascular dementia, high blood pressure, acute arthritis, multiple joint replacement surgeries, and finally, a second, more tragic fall.

Through it all, I thought that I was simply being a good daughter. My mom had been a source of support and inspiration all my life. I was just paying her back, doing what I was supposed to do as a loving daughter, but also what I wanted to do as a person with strong feelings about family, about moral obligations and duty. Nevertheless, I had no idea that I had slipped into a category of service, a little discussed way of life that had its own identity, a specific name, a role that is a world apart from what most of us regard as "normal." It wasn't until I took a cruise in January of 2011 that I discovered the name for what I was doing: *caregiving*. A light bulb moment that happened on a ship adrift at sea provided the perspective I needed to see myself in a different way. I was a family-based caregiver.

The details of family-based caregiving are different in each case because every aspect of the caregiving arrangement is unique to the individuals and families involved. That's what makes the problems associated with family-based care such a hard nut to crack. The home is a very private place. That is a big part of the problem. There is very little sharing among family caregivers.

Desperate for advice about how to properly handle my declining mother at home, I searched in vain for reference materials and guidance. I could find very little that helped me gain a better grasp of the day-to-day situations, tasks, resources, and skills that would make my caregiving efforts more effective and less stressful. Most of the available information consisted of writing by professionals and academics aimed at people like themselves, or well-meaning "support groups" that sympathetically address the emotional and psychological toll family caregivers commonly suffer but provide little in the way of useful tools or personal empowerment. This lack of focused, hands-on attention to the vital work performed by family caregivers could cripple our health care delivery system and cause needless suffering as our population enters an era of peak aging.

According to the U.S. Census nearly ten thousand people in this country turn sixty-five *every day*. My mother is a member of the "Greatest Generation," the

Depression era babies that came of age during World War II. In relative terms that has turned out to be a small group of elderly people. My generation, the baby boomers, is something else again. There are about 74 million of us. The country is about to experience a huge wave of elderly people, many of whom will have extended periods during which they will require caregiver services. With so many elderly in the demographic pipeline and the country already straining under the cost of programs like Medicare and Medicaid, it seems almost certain that home-based caregiving by family and friends will explode in coming years.

When I say "caregiver" I mean informal, unpaid family members who are providing care, usually at home. According to the American Association of Retired Persons (AARP) there are already 34 million Americans who fall into this category, providing some amount of care for some period of time to a person over fifty years of age. I have been one of those people for more than twenty-five years. Millions of other families and individuals will face the rising challenge of caring for aging, dependent adults.

As I read and researched and made notes about my own caregiving experiences, I began to realize the toil and struggle that I was experiencing was not a unique, isolated phenomenon. It affects a huge chunk of our society—literally millions of individuals—and will soon affect millions more.

Most of those people, like myself, could not possibly anticipate the complexities and stresses of what lay ahead. I realized that if we are ever to achieve a "continuum of care" that provides truly comprehensive, high-quality support for the health and wellness of aging Americans, family-based care practices would have to be illuminated, caregivers better trained and better informed. That caregiving part of the household would have to be opened up. As far as caregiving is concerned, the home should not be a place of hidden, private struggle and suffering. The problems of family-based care for elders are not unique to any individual or family unit. They have become a massive challenge confronting our communities and our society.

This book is about a journey. It is my account of the complicated, demanding, frustrating—the physically and emotionally draining—work of being a caregiver to an aging adult. It is also an account of the joy and sense of reward that comes from discharging caregiving responsibilities in the right way. It describes in detail my experiences with the various professions, agencies, bureaucracies, business organizations, entitlement programs, and support groups that are engaged in the exploding field of elder care services. And, I offer my own "best practice" models for approaching the duty of caring for an aging parent or loved one. It is hard won advice born of firsthand experience in an industry that has for the most part existed in the shadows of our society and our economy.

With tens of millions of Americans poised to enter the sunset of old age, it is time for us to have an open discussion about how we are going to manage to work, raise children, and have a life while also taking care of so many dependent aged. And we need to talk about how we are going to pay for it as well because the work required to properly and adequately support people in their declining years is very expensive in time and money.

It is my hope that this book proves valuable to family caregivers and to those who will become caregivers as well as to professionals, technicians, and service providers in the elder care industry. It is my effort to share some of the most intimate experiences accumulated over twenty-five years as a family caregiver, patient advocate, and hospice volunteer. These are the perceptions, thoughts, and notions I have amassed over that time. They have until now been personal and private—my secrets. By sharing I hope to inspire other caregivers to do the same, to communicate and network, to collaborate in establishing best practices and sensible standards that will make our efforts more productive, and more beneficial for the care recipient, with less wear and tear on the care provider. If it does that, it will make a useful contribution to the larger discussion of caregiving in our aging society, and well worth all the effort required to make it happen.

CHAPTER 1
Assuming the Role

Every caregiving situation has a backstory. As I said earlier, my mom and I had been very close as I grew up. From as far back as I can remember we were close. Many of the things that define my character came directly from her: a strong moral sense separating right from wrong; a love of stylish, beautiful things; a taste for southern cooking and cuisine; my sense of duty and commitment. Mom was a small woman, slim and petite with cocoa skin, wide eyes and a quiet manner. She was full of physical grace, always carrying herself as "a lady," although as was usual for a 1960s housewife, a plain cotton dress was her typical adornment. Mom loved to dance and one of my favorite memories was watching her and my father move smoothly across our living room floor in perfect rhythm to their favorite big band tunes. In due course I graduated from high school and matriculated to a state university a couple of hours from our hometown.

It was while I was in college that the unthinkable happened. My father, the respected principal of a local school, ran off to California. For me it was the equivalent of the sky falling. Like most young adults, I knew my parents' marriage wasn't perfect, but I thought that despite its various troubles, it was certain to endure. Not so. The abandonment put Mom in a bad spot

15

socially and financially. Ours was a small town where everybody knew everybody. Both my parents were natives of the area, deeply grounded with family and civic connections. My father's leaving upended Mom's life. Well into her fifties Mom for the first time had to go out and work a job to provide for her own survival. She had been a housewife forever and had no work skills to speak of.

Eventually Mom was hired as a switchboard operator by the local telephone utility. This was in the early 1970s, just when the telephone industry was starting to shift from analog to more modern digital technologies. Although she worked there for a number of years—long enough to earn a small pension—it was inevitable that the job would eventually be eliminated. She enjoyed the work and camaraderie there, but switchboards were technological dinosaurs, headed for extinction. When she was finally laid off, Mom, for a time, seemed to be managing all right. Meanwhile I had been married, gotten divorced, and was now busy raising my daughter. Although I stayed in touch with my mother, even visiting her apartment fairly often, I somehow missed the extent to which her financial circumstances were deteriorating.

By the time it dawned on me that my mother needed help, the situation was urgent. Mom was having trouble paying her utilities and rent. At first my siblings and I sought to subsidize her income with personal donations, but that didn't work out. It simply wasn't a consistent or adequate stream of revenue. There was a "family discussion" about what to do. Although I was the sibling with the greatest burden—single mom, stressful job, battling a chronic illness—it soon became clear that the burden of housing my mother would fall to me. But that was OK. I loved her. She was my mom.

I have a completely bald head. Clean as an egg. And I got it the hard way. In my late twenties while married and living with my husband and young daughter in Atlanta, Georgia, I was diagnosed with Crohn's disease. While not normally physically disabling the disease is debilitating, taking a huge toll on body and spirit over time including the alopecia that removed my head full of reddish-brown hair. Also, especially in the early years symptoms were treated with powerful steroids. Before being diagnosed I dealt with "flare-ups" in a state of pain and terror: my gut was on fire and I did not know what to do about it. Also, because Crohn's is a disease of the digestive tract, its many aspects are not usually discussed in our culture. This alone is enough to make it a condition out of bounds for polite discussion. So while people converse easily about truly terrible diseases like cancer or Alzheimer's, few feel comfortable discussing a condition that can involve rectal pain, chronic fatigue, and inflamed skin.

My years of coping with these aspects of Crohn's prepared me for many of the situations I experienced in family-based caregiving. Like the unpleasant symptoms of Crohn's, family-based caregiving is something almost everyone knows exists, but the implications are so unappealing that the subject is usually confined to a dark corner of the public mind. Just think about it. When you walk down the aisle of your big box chain drug store featuring dozens of treatments for indigestion, gas, bloating, constipation, diarrhea, hemorrhoids, and other delicate conditions, who do you think are users of these products? And why are there so many of them? Being ignored doesn't mean something isn't widespread. Issues with digestion and elimination are big problems in our population. People with chronic gastrointestinal distress live in these aisles. Family caregivers find themselves in a similar dilemma—dealing with commonplace but largely unacknowledged challenges.

Family-based care for the elderly often involves assisting the cared-for person with bathing and personal hygiene, toileting, dressing, and undressing, and any number of other high-touch activities. In the case of incontinence it can actually involve changing adult diapers and related cleanup, a distinctly unpleasant bit of work no matter how close one may be to the care recipient. And then there is the sense of embarrassment or shame often felt by those who must rely on others to perform these basic tasks. So between caregiver and recipient there can emerge a bond of silence. The caregiver is reluctant to admit administering these services, and the recipient is reluctant to admit needing them. This tacit bond is dangerous because it can affect other important aspects of care: conformity to medical protocols, compliance with diet, exercise or therapy, and so on. Too often what goes on within the family and within the caregiving household is regarded as highly personal and inaccessible to outsiders, including those providing primary medical care and other critical services. This is the unseen, protected, secret world of family caregiving that needs to open up.

The functional relationship between family caregiver and care recipient can be very sketchy. Most often it is predicated on an existing relationship; in my case, mother and daughter. For years that is how I related to my mother in our care relationship—as her daughter. But as time went by and my responsibilities grew, I began to give serious thought to whether the family caregiver role ought to be separate and apart from the blood relationship. In other words, I began to realize the caregiving role carried more weight because the daughter part, while a cherished emotional bond, was secondary to my identity as a caregiver.

Throughout the elder care industry the most important caregiving functions are based not on blood relationships and casual personal agreements, but legal standing and formally recognized powers. In most cases where a person is ill for example, a medical team will consult with "the family" about a patient's treatment options, but the possession of a power of attorney or healthcare power of attorney is the legal standard for acting on that person's behalf.

When I started thinking of myself less as a daughter taking care of her mother and more as a person with significant responsibilities toward a vulnerable person that I loved and cared about, everything shifted. That shift was caused by my mother designating me as her financial agent. Accepting appointment as agent under a power of attorney is a significant responsibility, especially in a family situation where there may be sibling rivalries that can create "Monday morning quarterbacking" of decisions. Fortunately my mom, realizing that she was declining, sat down with me and my older brother to work out an arrangement that covered her needs while minimizing possible family conflict. Of the four children born to my parents, only my older brother and I were available for these roles. An older sister had died a few years earlier, and a younger brother lived out west, far away, and was battling his own health problems.

Having a discussion about "what to do in case something happens" is probably the most important conversation members of a family can have. I am grateful that my mother had the foresight and took the time to have that discussion with my brother and me. Because my mother lived with me I was familiar with her personal life, including details of her medical and financial affairs. My older brother was better suited for evaluating critical issues related to health and wellness, including options for medical treatment. Mom named him her health care agent. The durable power of attorney and the health care power of attorney are two separate and distinct directives represented by two different legal documents. Once Mom decided who would have what responsibility, we had the legal papers drawn up and executed.

It cannot be emphasized enough the importance of having the right "paper" in place if one is to serve effectively as a family-based caretaker. In fact, all the relationships and interactions a caregiver handles on behalf of the care recipient are wrapped in reams and reams of paper. The durable power of attorney and the healthcare power of attorney are basic documents that allow designated persons to act in certain general situations. Medical institutions as well as state and other government agencies may have their own requirements and procedures that are often recorded with specialized documents. All this paper (now often in the form of electronic records) is important. Unless the family is wealthy enough to have a lawyer handle every single representation and transaction on behalf of a care recipient, it usually falls to the family caregiver to be an official record keeper. Apart from direct, hands-on assistance, maintaining accurate records and archiving documents is probably the most important caregiver role. In the whole discussion of caregiving and its many tasks, this vitally important function is often overlooked. (See the "Reader Resources" provided at the end of the book.)

Frankly, splitting the durable power of attorney and the health care power of attorney between my brother and me was from my point of view, an awkward arrangement. Several times, because I was the one who transported my mother to the emergency room when she was having one crisis or another, my lack of health care authority caused moments of anxiety. If my brother was traveling, or just not reachable by phone I could find myself in a quandary. But a family has to make compromises that address important needs while also keeping the peace among its members. Within our family unit, splitting the two powers was the solution my mother was most comfortable with.

What is the best way to determine whom within the family exercises these important powers? That may vary for each family based on factors from personalities and existing conflicts among members, to considerations of education, professional background, and other relevant experience. The caregiver need not necessarily hold these "power" roles as well. A person's willingness and ability to perform should be key considerations. Some family members will not want the responsibility. Nothing is worse than giving a job to a person who doesn't want it and who winds up not doing it well or not doing it at all. Probably the best scenario is the one my family experienced: have the person who will be subject to care simply designate who does what, with those persons being willing and able to take on the tasks. That may not satisfy everyone; that is, it may not eliminate resentments and griping, but it is authoritative.

It should be noted that in many states, including my state of North Carolina, a hierarchy of decision makers established by statute determines who represents an incapable person if there is no health care power of attorney. This hierarchy begins with a living spouse then moves on to adult parents and children. If there is conflict among persons of equal standing, such as two children who disagree about a plan of care, decision-making can become difficult. In such a case, having a designated decision maker through a health care power of attorney can help reduce or eliminate conflict. If an incapacitated patient has only one child, for example, that person will be able to exercise health care decision making by law and a health care power of attorney will not be needed. State laws vary on these matters. It is important to know the laws of your state.

The "shift" I refer to—moving from dutiful daughter to formal caregiver—was an epiphany for me. Although for years I had been accompanying my mom to doctors' appointments, dashing her to urgent care, monitoring medical payments and making co-payments, comforting her through hospitalizations, filling prescriptions, and performing the dozens of other everyday caregiver tasks, I never added it all up. With the power of attorney and eventually the financial guardianship I was also granted, it eventually occurred to me that my mother was one of many small cogs in a big system—this country's system of care for the elderly. It is a big, cumbersome, disjointed, often dysfunctional system. And, it is a business.

That is one of the main arguments for encouraging family-based care whenever it is possible. Caregiving by employees, although important and honorable work, is like most kinds of low-status employment, just a job— low paying, and without benefits, advancement opportunities or incentives to excel. Many do that job as well as they can, but often it is not enough.

My mom was in a wide range of care institutions— hospitals, rehab, assisted living, and a nursing facility. Some were highly rated and connected to prestigious institutions, some not so much. One thing I observed is that regardless of the ranking or prestige or reputation of a facility, nobody takes care of a person better than those by whom they are loved and cherished. In institutions, no matter how reputable, there are always cracks people can fall through. There are bureaucratic entanglements and crazy rules and "Catch 22" nonsense.

Family-based care is far from perfect. Its biggest shortcoming is that this country does not have family leave policies and support programs that allow better planning and implementation of care by relatives. And there is far too little training and education offered to family care providers. More systematic outreach, training, and technical support could make them a strong link in the "continuum of care" most experts in this country believe we will need to weather the demographic storm now underway.

Armed mostly with my own experience navigating the health care system and a lot of good intentions, I began my journey as a family-based caregiver to an increasingly fragile and dependent parent. Along the way I would get a close-up look at what I now think of as the eldercare industry. Family-based care is just a big, underappreciated, and often unacknowledged component of that industry. It is a component that needs to be lifted up, nurtured, and developed to its full potential. That would be a win for everyone: caregivers, the elders they care for, communities, and the country as a whole.

These are among the first "principles of family caregiving" that I learned:

- Have caregiving conversations with likely care recipients sooner rather than later. The conversations become more awkward and difficult with the passage of time.

- Caregiving is increasingly focused on *coordination of care*—making and keeping appointments, managing communications among various medical providers, monitoring and providing feedback on treatment outcomes, etc. The role requires the ability to juggle tasks, focus on details, organizational skills, and a boatload of patience.

- The caregiver's role is strengthened by a good knowledge of family medical history. Genetic tendencies and chronic illnesses tend to manifest over time. Don't lapse into denial by assuming you or any other family member will be an exception.

- Keep *copies* of all legal forms in a lock box. The durable power of attorney is of great importance. After completion and execution it should be recorded in your county's public records. Original health care documents (living will, durable health care power of attorney, advance directives) should be kept in a place that is readily accessible—not in your safe deposit box.

- Keep a complete and current record of contact information for health care providers—doctors, clinics, pharmacies, etc. — including telephone numbers and website passwords. Do not try to keep this information in your head. It is an added stressor and you're likely to forget or misremember the information in emergency situations.

- Use the CareZone app or something similar on your smartphone to track medications.

- Learn how to access and frequently update your knowledge of the care recipient's electronic medical records. Ask the doctor about entries that are unfamiliar. The ability to reference data in medical records can make a big difference when communicating with doctors and hospital staff, especially in emergencies.
- Make sure health care documents are part of the care recipient's medical record.
- Be conversant about what is "normal" for the care recipient—baseline vital signs.
- Be prepared to ask family for help or develop a relationship with an agency for care by the hour/day/week for a special social event or much needed vacation. Accept that some plans should be tentative. Establish a routine of being away from the care recipient on occasion so that expectations don't become unreasonable. Be firm about your need for respite even if there is resistance.

CHAPTER 2
The Patient Advocate

The family-based caregiver has many roles, including: monitoring care plans with providers; medication management; assistance with activities of daily living; arranging medical appointments; shopping, meals, and transportation. Sometimes those roles can bleed into each other causing confusion and even a kind of psychological paralysis. You just don't know what to do. That's why it was important for me to mentally separate my role as daughter from the formal responsibilities I assumed toward my mother as caregiver. This was hard to do on a day-to-day basis, but it was necessary. I found that decisions made in the emotional heat of my feelings as a daughter often turned out badly or did not get the outcome I wanted. On the other hand when I thought through a problem, did my research, evaluated the other players in a situation, and made moves that were informed and calculated, good things usually happened. In the home I was my mother's primary caregiver, but as my mother aged and her medical conditions became more acute, a great deal of her care came from outside the home—from doctors, hospitals, and specialized service providers such as geriatricians, endocrinologists, cardiologists, physical therapists, and rheumatologists. My manner of interacting with these people was different from my mother's. She was the patient; I was her advocate. She was receiving care; I was monitoring the quality and appropriateness of that care. The distinction may seem obvious, but it often isn't obvious to caregivers.

The role required that I focus exclusively on her needs, and be responsive to her concerns. It required that I provide encouragement and comfort as well as reminders about sticking to the choices and routines recommended by doctors and other health care providers. I worked to ensure that she understood directives given by medical personnel during office visits or hospital stays, as well as posed to medical providers' questions she had brought up at home, but may have forgotten by the time of an appointment. Being an advocate also required that I ensured she was always involved in her health care decisions, that her voice was heard in the doctor's office, the hospital, or the care facility. Without that element of respect and inclusion, it is hard to achieve the level of compliance needed for a high quality of life despite health related challenges.

One of the family caregiver's most difficult but essential jobs is to serve as an effective patient advocate. In my case that meant guiding my mother through the often confusing maze of our health care system with the sensitivity that family members seem best able to provide. As my mother's advocate I focused exclusively on her needs and responded to her concerns. My responsibility was to keep her at the center of all decision-making regarding her health and wellness, and to help achieve the highest level of compliance with the goals and practices established by her health plan.

My own medical history proved helpful in organizing my thinking about planning for and managing Mom's medical care. In addition to wrangling with the Crohn's disease for decades—which brought about serious bone and joint damage from medications as well as a bowel resection—I have endured multiple surgeries including replacement of both knees, elbow surgery, carpel tunnel release surgery on both hands, and shoulder surgery. These surgical episodes required extensive hospital stays, interactions with many types of medical practitioners, therapists, and other specialists. My various conditions required a wide range of medicines and I had to be very aware of the dangers of side effects and interactions. Therefore I made a special effort to become familiar and conversational with my medical providers and learn their language.

For much of the period during which I experienced my most intense medical treatments, I was a single mom. When there was a doctor's appointment I drove to it myself. Crohn's patients require frequent colonoscopies, which are outpatient type procedures done at outpatient surgical centers under sedation. After the procedure the patient is pretty out of it, drowsy and disoriented. Most clinics require that a patient be accompanied by a driver to avoid the risks of driving themselves while still under the influence of the sedative. Patients are instructed not to drive for twenty-four hours after the procedure, but if you don't have anyone to call on to drive you, there is no other option but to sit in the waiting room until your head clears enough that you feel able to drive, or go out to the parking deck and sit in the car until sensibility returns. As alarming as this seems in retrospect, I did it several times. The medical team was unaware of this of course; they were sincerely concerned about my having a safe trip home.

As I experienced, the circumstances of an individual patient don't always align with proper medical protocol. This is one of the biggest points of separation between "clinical" medical practice and the realities of a person's life. The advice and recommendations of medical personnel are framed by clinical assumptions. Life *outside* the clinic is anything but clinical. Most clinical personnel (doctors, nurses, technicians) are fairly well paid and live reasonably comfortable if not affluent lifestyles. They or their place of employment may naturally assume that "everyone" can arrange for a ride home. But "everyone" can't. Those who cannot, do what they have to do. This is a scenario repeated time and time again in the family caregiving realm. Outside hospitals and doctors' offices "clinical" practices and assumptions can quickly fall apart. Real life intervenes. Instructing someone that they "have to" do this thing to be consistent with medical protocol means nothing if the person simply cannot do the recommended thing.

Sometimes a patient doesn't even have to leave the medical facility to experience the rupture between formal treatment and reality. During the numerous occasions when I was in recovery after surgeries or having a particularly nasty flare-up of Crohn's and taking strong medication, I could find myself for all intents and purposes incapacitated, yet still conferencing with doctors and medical personnel. Although I might have been able to make out their questions and even respond in a satisfactory way, it was impossible for me to process everything being said let alone retain any important information that may have been exchanged. Memories of being by myself in vulnerable situations where critical discussions of a medical nature were taking place helped shape my approach to serving as an advocate for Mom.

And then there was my friend diagnosed with breast cancer in her forties. It was treated to remission and she went on to have a successful career in the corporate world. But in her fifties the cancer returned, this time in a different organ. During the friend's struggle to turn back this threat, I accompanied her to appointments and other sessions, taking notes, sharing thoughts, and helping maintain her spirits. In this role of support I learned even more about the inner workings of the medical industry and the needs of vulnerable patients— those heavily medicated, suffering excruciating pain, or simply immobilized by the terror of their situations—to have someone in their corner, providing moral support and looking out for their interests. Later I became a volunteer advocate for and companion to other cancer patients. All this was good training, enabling me to better take care of my mom as her health began to deteriorate.

Why did my mom need an attentive, critical, and committed advocate? There are a number of reasons. First of all my mom is from a different generation. The culture in which she came to adulthood emphasized obedience to authority figures, and doctors were iconic figures of authority. That is not to say that Mom lacked the ability to challenge guidance or decisions she found questionable, it's just that the cultural norms she embraced discouraged such behavior. As she grew older Mom had a long list of ailments. An irregular heartbeat necessitated the implanting of a pacemaker. For years she had suffered high and sometimes wildly variable blood pressure. She had severe arthritis and endured four hip replacement operations, including three on the right side, one on the left. Her low heart rate eventually contributed to vascular dementia, which could make her forgetful, confused, or disoriented. Mom could be feisty and quick to take offense. And, she was hard of hearing. These things could create tension. I usually accompanied my mom to her medical appointments and treatments. I took notes, asked questions, and had the opportunity to observe. As her primary caregiver I learned to listen closely, read between the lines of exchanges, and explain to Mom things she might not have fully comprehended, in an effort to head off misunderstandings before they escalated into more serious problems.

One of the first things I noticed during my mother's appointments was how medical personnel can be unobservant and tone deaf. Medicine is a volume business and personnel see many of the same conditions over and over. So it is understandable that a kind of rote behavior might set in. I was surprised that many of the professionals working with my mother could not pick up on visual and other clues that she was hard of hearing. They would be chattering along as mom leaned practically out of her chair with the hearing aid aimed directly at them, yet at no time would they ask or verify that she understood everything they said. Thankfully I was there, usually taking notes. Had my mom been in many of those sessions either alone or with a less interested companion, a great deal of important information and guidance would likely have been lost. This missing information could have directly affected her health outcomes.

There were other issues. Many times we would arrive for an appointment and it was obvious that the provider had not read Mom's medical chart. Medical offices, clinics and hospitals are busy places. While we enter these establishments under the spell of an ideal—that of the Hippocratic oath—it is easy to forget that these places are businesses and are operated as businesses. Attention to detail takes time, and time is money. That's why serving as a patient advocate is so important. It requires attentiveness as well as some measure of preparation, which usually comes from accumulated knowledge and excellent record keeping. These are keys to monitoring the quality of care being provided to the care recipient.

Medical personnel may be highly skilled in their fields, but they often work in isolation from each other. The point at which all their efforts converge to create a measurable result is the medical chart, the best running tab on a patient's wellbeing. In caregiving, someone always needs to be observing the efforts of medical providers and monitoring the chart in the best interests of the patient. As my mom's primary caregiver that job fell to me. An important innovation and excellent tool for monitoring medical conditions and quality of care in real time is electronic medical records. As soon as the technology was available I established online access to medical charts for myself and my mom. Unlike old paper files, online charts are readily accessible to the patient as well as the medical provider. Patients and their authorized helpers have access to some of the same information that the people treating them do, and are therefore on a more equal footing with providers, able to ask informed questions with the facts and background to make sense of answers.

For example, for years before online records were available I would hear Mom ask about lab results and have her question dismissed with a wave of the hand, along with the comment that her labs were fine. Well, maybe they were. But medical records are not always accurate. And lab results are usually ranked within a statistical range that is considered "normal." Saying results are fine may indicate they fall within the normal range, but it doesn't reveal important information—such as whether numbers are, over time, trending up or down or are noticeably variable. Pulling up the online records I could review test results—and our respective medical histories—at home at a time convenient to me. If I noticed anything concerning I could make a note to bring it up at our next appointment, or if things seemed really out of kilter, email a note to the doctor through the online records network.

Online records really empower patients and their caregivers and advocates. They are great tools for giving patients timely information about their health status, and for correcting errors that may find their way into the record. But some basic skills are required to use them productively. Having pored over my own paper records for years, the transition to online data was easy for me. Providing educational support to patients and their caregivers about navigating and understanding this personal medical database is I think one of the great needs that currently exists in medicine and particularly among family-based caregivers.

Older people can be inordinately stubborn. "Set in their ways," is one way to describe it. My mother, though outwardly gentle and compliant, could also be rigidly uncooperative. At one point she had a primary care physician who I thought was not paying adequate attention to her deteriorating physical and mental state.

But he had a charming "bedside manner," and Mom was quite taken with him. After researching alternative practices, I settled on one that I thought would be an excellent replacement. But when I brought this up with Mother, she bristled. As her caregiver, I was focused mainly on the quality of care being provided. But my mom was more focused on the relationship that was developing between her and the physician. She liked him. That was the most important thing. It took several very unpleasant encounters and several months before I was finally able to convince her to make the change. This is one of the instances in which the separation of daughter from caregiver proved useful. I knew remaining at that practice was not in Mom's best interest, yet she was determined not to leave. I had to be patient, yet insistent, collecting evidence to support my view while preventing the resulting arguments from becoming personal. It was all about getting the best care. Eventually we managed to work out our differences. If as a daughter I simply wanted my mother to be happy, she would no doubt have remained in the care of that physician. But as her responsible caregiver I had to make the decision to change and convince Mom that my recommendation was preferable, even if it went against her wishes.

One of the issues that triggered this incident was my feeling that Mom was not receiving full disclosure and transparency in many of the treatment discussions. A discovery made when I first became involved with

Mom's medical care was that she didn't ask questions about medication. If it was prescribed, she bought it and took it. Her doctor did not always volunteer the most basic information—length of treatment, possible side effects, drug and food interactions, what to do in case of reactions, whether there was a less expensive generic brand, and whether the drug could be stopped cold or had to be tapered.

By default, I ended up asking these questions, which did not always please the physician, and made Mom uneasy. It wasn't that Mom disapproved of my asking the questions. She knew I was doing that in her best interests. But she tended to assume a compliant posture in the presence of an authority figure.

Related to this, when Mom went to the doctor, she tended to put on her best face. It was as though she sought to please the doctor—to ensure him she was doing as well as he expected. It was my duty to reveal the not-so-sanguine details of her many sufferings. She wanted the doctor to believe she was getting better, and perhaps to make herself believe the same thing by psyching herself up for the appointment. But in the final analysis putting on the best face was self-defeating. The physician needed to know the truth about her condition—complete and unvarnished.

I ended up coaching her about what to say and how to respond to questions I knew would likely be asked. Care relationships, especially those forged with busy, sometimes tunnel-visioned medical personnel are delicate things. Over time Mom and I became sensitized to the moods, attitudes, and body language of the professional and technical specialists we worked with. We found that the quality of attention and counsel we received was often directly related to our own tone and demeanor. We found that quality of care was more or less correlated with perceptions of our willingness to accept their authority without question. This didn't offend us. We knew that the personnel serving us saw dozens of people every day. They had protocols to observe, management directives to follow, and business objectives to achieve. Somewhere within that web of regulations and controls and pressures we land as patients.

Herein lies the value of the patient advocate role. The medical system is extremely complex and layered. It is in a state of almost continuous upheaval due to structural changes to medical practice and related industries. There are rapid technology innovations. Rule changes and policy shifts by the big payment sources—Medicare, Medicaid, and private insurers—occur with regularity. There is a lot to know, a lot to keep up with, and nobody can know or keep up with it all. But two heads are much better than one, especially if the one head is the patient herself—scared, medicated, often in pain, and intimidated by the sheer scale of modern medicine as an industry.

That's why I realized it wasn't enough just to be a dutiful daughter taking care of Mom. She needed a home-based caretaker, for sure, but she also needed an informed, capable advocate, someone to recognize and protect her interests in the sometimes murky and disingenuous world of elder care. So on my own, I set out to make myself that person. It helped enormously that we had done one thing right. We had sat down as a family and decided upon roles. A family caretaker— me—had been formally designated and the necessary legal "paper" was in place—power of attorney, financial guardianship, health care power of attorney, last will and testament. I didn't know exactly what was coming, but it felt as though I had some tools to work with as well as my mother's blessing. With the latter of course being more important than anything else.

Being a family caregiver can be an enormous burden, psychologically, physically, and financially. Much of the writing and discussion I have encountered on the subject is more concerned with the damage caretaking responsibility does to individuals giving it than the benefits family-based care provides its recipients. Those concerns are well founded. Caretaking can wear a person down to almost nothing. It can be a killer. On the other hand being a family caretaker can be hugely rewarding.

I will never forget an especially dark period when Mom wasn't doing well and I was having repeated flare-ups with my own chronic illness. None of my ordinary stresses—working and managing a household for instance—paused when health care crises arose. My anxieties simply doubled or tripled or quadrupled.

During this particular episode, I was nearly beside myself with worry and frustration.

I had taken Mom to an appointment. It may have been one of the periodic checks on her arthritis or hip replacements. I can't remember. At any rate Mom was out of the examining room having an X-ray or some other procedure done and I was sitting there alone, considering all the challenges I faced. A doctor came in. He was holding Mom's chart and had evidently been reading through it. We started discussing Mom's precarious health and prospects. Suddenly, it all poured out. The dam broke. Every bit of disappointment, anger, resentment, and lack of appreciation I felt as a caregiver came out in a torrent. The doctor just sat there, calm, erect, and attentive. When I was done and feeling the full weight of embarrassment, he was quite still, his head tilted slightly in thought. Then he leaned toward me, elbows on knees, his mouth lifting at the corners, almost smiling. Our eyes locked. Then he spoke: "You are the main reason your mother is still alive."

The words froze me. I couldn't speak. My mind raced around all I had been thinking and saying, then inevitably returned to that single amazing declaration. It was as though a missing piece in my caregiving puzzle had been snapped into place. I realized that—other than Mom's explicit gratitude—much of my frustration actually stemmed from a lack of recognition, a refusal by the world to acknowledge my extraordinary efforts. Then in one simple sentence all of that resentment dissolved. In a single moment I understood what I was doing and why. From that point forward, regardless of challenges and difficulties, I was never more appreciative of having my mother in my life, of enjoying her companionship, her existence. And it all spun off a single comment by a thoughtful, kind, and very wise physician.

Dealing with physicians and other situations in the health care system can be complicated, tricky work. Here are some tips:

- In healthcare situations, calm, clear, precise communication is extremely important. Stick to the facts. Being argumentative is counterproductive.

- Expressions of impatience and frustration can sow seeds of distrust between caregiver and care recipient.

- Lower your expectations. Elderly care recipients are often medicated. They may be forgetful or confused. Don't ask questions that can be interpreted as challenges or insults, such as, "Don't you remember?"

- Until such time that cognitive impairment or physical decline dictate otherwise, try to involve the care recipient in all aspects of care planning and decision-making.

- Efficient management of appointments is vital. It reduces frustration and wasted time. Use your smartphone to manage the care recipient's appointments as well as your own personal calendar to avoid overbooking and to reduce conflicts. Remember that schedule managers at clinics and other providers are very busy. Be polite and ready to explain your situation when rescheduling. Keep a large monthly calendar in the home, posted in a prominent location (like the laundry room door) as a visible reminder.
- When relying on a third party for transportation or other assistance, make sure the commitment is firm. Don't make arrangements based on what someone else *might* be able to do.

CHAPTER 3
Family is as Family Does

Having been active in caretaking circles for about a quarter century, I have met and talked to enough people to know that every caretaking story is different. Every set of family circumstances that creates the need for a caretaking arrangement is different. This is in part what leads family caretakers to view their lot as unknowably unique and completely unlike anyone else's burden. After all their family isn't like anyone else's family and no one could possibly understand all the factors and complexities that make their family the way it is. This is the wall family-based caretakers tend to build around themselves, and it is intended to protect the family as much as it provides for care to the needy member. As caregivers, they can become more and more inwardly focused, take on more and more responsibility, and become more and more overextended. Often they become more and more exhausted, depleted, beaten down, and unglued.

When Mom moved in with me we were both in the middle of our own personal financial crises. It was clear that she was struggling since her forced retirement; all around her the world of work had suddenly changed in a big way. Computers were taking over everything. Having little or no understanding of that emerging technology, plus already being in her mid-sixties, there were few employment opportunities available. Plus she had spent nearly all her adult years close to home, raising children and being a housewife. Beyond family and church she did not have a wide social network. Private and self-reliant, she was reluctant to suddenly engage the larger community and tap the various resources that might assist her.

But I was having my own problems. A spate of unexpected medical and other expenses had upset my budget, forcing me to move myself and my daughter from a nice brick townhome that I enjoyed in a neighborhood where I felt safe into a working class community overrun with single parent, female-headed households. To make ends meet I picked up a second job, meaning I would be away from home thirteen or fourteen hours a day. Then I learned that the lead researcher with whom I worked had been awarded a large grant that would require him to leave the university where we worked. I would have to find other full-time employment. From talking to my mom on the phone I knew she was in an even worse situation than mine. Something would have to be done about her situation or she would likely become destitute.

With a sense of foreboding, I drove the two hours south to see my mother, review her finances, and discuss her options. After a moment of embarrassment she spoke candidly, and it became clear that living separately, in her own place, was out of the question unless she received some outside financial help.

Knowing I could not handle Mom's cash shortfall on my own I called my local siblings for a family meeting, thinking we could figure out a way to pitch in and prop Mom up. From my calculations, if we all chipped in $50 to $100 a month, she would be able to stay in her apartment, remaining close to her small circle of family and friends. While providing a small monthly subsidy for Mom was not a mandatory obligation for any of us, it seemed to me to be the most reasonable and cost effective alternative available. I was not willing to watch our mother suffer a series of setbacks that would surely leave her bankrupt when we, her children, had the means to achieve a different outcome. The situation resolved with Mom and me packing up her apartment, putting some things into storage, and starting the process of figuring out how to live together.

Honestly, the idea of refusing to help my mother never crossed my mind. Still, I had many concerns about how that transition would be managed. Adding a person to an established household can be disruptive, and my teenaged daughter and I were close, many of our interactions so familiar that they were basically automatic. I knew that bringing Mom into the fold was bound to change our household chemistry.

When she moved in with us, I expected Mom to contribute to our household financially, be a presence when my daughter came home from school, and help with household chores. I also expected her to become involved in community activities, and plan for her future. My thought was that our cohabitation would be temporary, brought on by her strained finances. Once she got her life restructured and became more financially stable, I expected she would move on. But that wasn't my mother's plan. Because her move was wrapped in all the confusion and impulsive action that comes with crisis management, I failed to pay sufficient attention to the details that would govern our arrangement. This resulted in many awkward and painful experiences.

After she settled in, Mom was reluctant to discuss her finances, her choices and her future. I suspect she was mildly depressed for many years, although I have no way of verifying that. The marital divide and subsequent departure of my father was devastating for Mom and left her with meager financial resources. Her way of coping was to steel herself against many things, including the hum of small town gossip. Out of necessity, she had developed her own fractured way of coping and managing her household. She brought those inclinations along with her. Losing her job at the telephone company was an embarrassing setback; it prevented her from reaching out for help sooner. Years later she would recall the name of the person who delivered the news and her paralyzing embarrassment at being told she would be laid off. With my patience compromised by working two jobs, raising my daughter, and managing a chronic illness, tensions escalated. Instead of her presence bringing financial relief, I continued working two jobs to meet the mounting expenses. But to be clear, Mom never said she would be making a significant financial contribution to the household; that was my unspoken expectation.

Many days I had to hold my tongue so I didn't say anything that destroyed our relationship. Usually, I steadied myself and controlled the frustration by asking, "How would I want to be treated if I were her age, forced into retirement and unable to pay my bills?" In some unexamined but compelling way, I felt responsible for her. I certainly wasn't going to put her out, and by working two jobs didn't have to give up much of a social life. Each time I thought about applying hard stops to her behavior, it seemed spiteful and petty. I spent many nights thinking about the position I was in and the lack of meaningful assistance from my family.

Like many family caregivers, I had been thrust into an arrangement I was not prepared to handle. What began as a well-intentioned, impromptu effort to solve a family crisis evolved into a more permanent dependency over time as Mom's health gradually began to slip. Before we got to the years of greater dependency, I had to survive the ordeal of integrating her into my household. My initial response was avoidance. I tried to minimize conflict, deflect provocations, and be as accommodating as I could. In time the energy to sustain that behavior ran out. I overcorrected and started treating mother like my child. There was no transition, no plan; the thought process was flawed. Adjustments were just made on the

49

fly, rising up out of circumstance, desperation, and frustration.

Because I worked so much my teenage daughter was a latchkey kid, arriving home from school to an empty house where she was on her own. That situation caused me constant worry. Another adult in the home would in that sense be a blessing. Having Mom around could enrich my daughter's life in other ways. She could pick up historical perspective from listening to her grandmother's accounts of past events and how things had changed over time. Her connections to members of the extended family would be strengthened by Mom's penchant for frequent visits to relatives. And I believed my daughter would gain a better understanding of me by coming to know the woman who raised me. All in all the upside of having an intergenerational family appeared to outweigh the downside.

Much too late, I realized Mom and I had not thought through our cohabitation with the thoroughness and attention to detail it required. We had not talked about and agreed on ground rules governing her contribution to household expenses, expectations of privacy, and other boundaries. Roles were not clearly defined. I treated my mother like a roommate, and she treated me like a daughter. Though not always obvious, the move to my place created trauma for Mom. Her sense of loss of independence and autonomy was palpable, and could show itself in odd ways—such as efforts at exerting authority. She didn't hesitate to express when I wasn't meeting her expectations, such as being available for sit-down dinners and regular church attendance. Hey, I was working two jobs. That just wasn't going to happen. Most importantly I learned that my failure to discuss the length of her stay was problematic. It never occurred to me that my mother would not want to live on her own again. As a relatively young woman, I was OK with Mom sharing my household for a transitional period of time, but I didn't anticipate her becoming a permanent dependent.

There was other fallout. Mom's arrival caused some household expenses to increase, including utilities and the phone bill because at that time long distance calls were billed separately and by the minute. Understandably she wanted to stay in touch with family and friends. There were also differences in diet and eating habits I didn't anticipate. While Mom had a couple of sources of fixed and limited, but steady income, and I had some idea of her disposable funds, I was reluctant to make demands.

It was also a challenge to protect my time with my daughter and Mom grew resentful of my efforts to protect our privacy. I did not want my daughter to be overwhelmed by the demands of answering to "two mothers," wary of the potential for conflicting guidance and confusion inherent in that. My fatigue and lack of resources began to magnify even the smallest differences.

All that is to say that the circumstances under which I came to serve initially as a safety net for my mother, and that eventually led to my becoming her family caregiver, were indeed unique to my family's circumstances. But the uniqueness was of degree, not of kind. Every family caregiver has a comparable "origin story," and no two are exactly alike. Differences in details about the origin of their caregiving duties cannot minimize the shared dilemmas and challenges faced by all family caregivers. Recognition of how much is shared—that much of their plight is rooted in social rather than private factors—is probably the key to improving family caregivers' understanding of their important social contribution as well as improving the health outcomes of the individuals they provide for.

As with most middle-aged people I had been through some challenges by the time my mother moved in, including picking up the pieces from a failed marriage and battling a persistent, draining chronic illness. I had learned to live in the world as a single parent juggling responsibilities for financial provision, homemaking, and parenting. Although steadily employed in good jobs, my greatest challenge was financial uncertainty. My greatest commitment was to my daughter—creating a foundation from which she could launch herself into the world successfully.

Being the primary breadwinner and head nurturer in my family allowed me to develop skills in problem solving, time management, and organization. Those roles also demanded patience, self-control, and empathy. This is a skill set ideally suited for caregiving and it is a source I draw from repeatedly in overcoming the twists, turns, and roadblocks that litter the caregiving landscape. Those like me, who take on the challenge of informal (meaning unpaid) caregiving have to acquire these abilities. The fate of their care recipient hangs in the balance.

It took a while for me to realize what lay ahead. From the start I knew Mom had at least one serious chronic medical issue, but I didn't grasp the extent to which I would need to involve myself in managing her health and wellness challenges. Initially, because she relocated far from her established business and professional relationships, she had to find new doctors and other healthcare providers. I helped her with that. For several years—through our lengthy period of household adjustment—Mom could go to the store, put gas in her car, and go to appointments alone. The turning point was her third of four hip replacement surgeries. After that surgery and recovery it seemed I was much more involved in helping her find doctors, fill prescriptions, repair her car, do shopping, and conduct many other every day, time-consuming tasks. In hindsight I should have seen it coming, but at the time felt blindsided. Just when I was fully engaged in my own very challenging life, I was faced with assuming increasing responsibility for a deteriorating parent.

After almost 20 years of caring for Mom, I was exhausted. A friend who thought I could use a break, mentioned an ocean cruise I might want to take. The trip was being marketed especially to "caregivers." I signed up. It was on this cruise I learned that the heightened emotions and stress levels that had recently enveloped my life were common to family caregivers and I needed to get a handle on them or I was on my way to a nervous breakdown. To my surprise I also learned that all the issues I was struggling with silently and in isolation were also quite common among caregivers, and the results I was experiencing were generally better than the usual outcomes. What I lacked in resources, time, and support I made up for in resilience, determination, persistence, and attention to detail. The cruise experience encouraged me to learn by reading, researching, attending workshops, and following leads. I opened up, putting my vulnerability on display. I learned not to fear saying, "I didn't know that." The secret to being sane in the family caregiving universe is to understand how and when and where to reach out for help. It took me a long time to understand that it is OK to ask for help. Every household is different. That makes the circumstances specific and each caregiving environment different. But there are some things everyone facing caregiving responsibilities can do to ease the transition for everyone involved:

- Many caregiving situations arise from sudden, unforeseen events. Often there is little or no time to think through the commitment. Before diving into the role, try to pause for a day or so. Take about 48 hours, if the situation allows. Consider how this undertaking might impact life as you know it. Jot down a few talking points to be discussed with other family members.

- Prepare yourself for a detailed discussion of roles, responsibilities, finances, and boundaries with the care recipient. Make a record of what is agreed upon.

- It would be wise to take my mother's advice when faced with a new challenge— start off in a way that you can continue; in other words, pace yourself.

CHAPTER 4
The Family Caregiver

One thing that I find curious and somewhat misleading is the frequent reference to generic "home caregiving." Whenever I talk about caregiving I am always careful to distinguish between caregiving services offered by commercial enterprises on-site in a person's home and the informal, unpaid caregiving services provided by loved ones, relatives, or friends. Both are "home caregiving," but the two things are not the same. For the past twenty-five years I have been an informal— which is to say unpaid—family caregiver. That is by far the largest category of home-based caregiving in terms of people engaged and the range of care services provided. In my case the level of care started at a relatively moderate level and grew in intensity as years passed. In the family caregiver's case, caregiving responsibility doesn't necessarily end when the recipient is moved to an institutional setting. At this writing my mother no longer lives with me, but resides in a twenty-four-hour skilled nursing facility. Her relocation hasn't necessarily curtailed my work; instead the load has just shifted in focus and moved "off site." More on that later.

Because I meandered into the role of family caregiver, for years I wasn't even aware that what I was doing had a name other than "taking care of mom." It wasn't like

Mom was the victim of a sudden health catastrophe such as a stroke or heart attack who unexpectedly and urgently needed the kind of support that would shock me into an awareness of the change in our relationship. Her decline was gradual and at first almost imperceptible. When my duties toward her began to multiply and intensify I was compelled to go in search of resources and relief. Fortunately I have worked most of my adult life at academic or teaching institutions—colleges, universities, and other levels of education. My work responsibilities often required that I exercise a great deal of independent initiative in solving problems. So I was accustomed to taking an analytical approach to challenges, doing unsupervised research, delving into the inner workings of things I knew little about, putting two and two together, and connecting dots.

Once I figured out that "caregiver" was the formal label for the work that I was doing my next step was to look into exactly what caregiving was all about. That quest for information took me to a mind-boggling range of sources weighing in on one or another aspect of the role, but the main thing I wanted was facts. I found those facts in a variety of places, but especially in a publication titled "Caregiving in the U.S.," survey research conducted by AARP and the National Alliance of Caregivers (stats cited in this chapter are from the survey). It amazed me that there were so many of us. For example, the 2015 report estimated that, "Approximately 34.2 million Americans have provided unpaid care to an adult age fifty or over in the prior twelve months." That is a really big number. And, according to the American Psychological Association, in as many as 1.4 million American households, children as young as nine and ten years old are caring for disabled elders, often with tragic consequences for their development.

So there I was, "taking care of mom" completely tunnel-visioned, my attention fixed only on the immediate responsibilities and crises in front of me, thinking my problems were singular and unique. Of course I was vaguely aware that many people care for disabled or aged loved ones. The thing is, I was thinking of those instances as separate and unconnected family issues, when in reality they constituted a huge, but almost hidden "body of work," that was basically an industry. And it dawned on me that the main reason family-based caregiving was invisible was because in most cases the people doing the work were not paid. The only other comparable I could come up with was housework, including raising children. The main thing the two jobs have in common—besides being unpaid— is that they are performed mostly by women.

Let me be clear. My decision to become caregiver to my mom had nothing to do with any expectation of being paid. Nor do I believe most family caregivers think in terms of their efforts as a job for which payment ought to be expected. For the most part, family caregivers are motivated by a bond of love or kinship or commitment to the person cared for. Statistics bear that out. "A large majority of caregivers provide care for a relative (85 percent), with 49 percent caring for a parent or parent-in-law." About 10 percent of caregivers are caring for a spouse or partner. These tend to be caregivers putting in the highest number of hours. In addition 10 percent of caregivers are seventy-five years of age or older! This is an amazing statistic. It means that there are millions of people in advanced old age who are themselves struggling to take care of other people.

The more I dug around in the massive, incredibly diverse mountain of information related to the various types of care provided to our elderly population, the more I came to regard the entire sector as a kind of strange, make-it-up-as-you-go-along, Rube Goldberg enterprise. A lot of things just didn't make sense. For example it has been known for decades that our country and the entire Western world would be facing the currently unfolding demographic crisis. It was known that rapidly aging populations would put extraordinary pressure on many parts of our social structure, and would especially impact the medical field. Then I noticed several news articles (such as the *New York Times* articles cited in sources), about how few geriatricians are being produced by the medical field despite the surging numbers of elderly individuals. In fact, geriatrics seems to be a medical specialty headed for extinction. I know firsthand because I have struggled to keep a quality geriatric specialist on Mom's list of medical providers. The problem? Seems that geriatrics doesn't pay as much as other specialties.

Just because work isn't paid doesn't mean it isn't valuable. This is particularly true of family-based caregiving. In its special report, "The $234 Billion Job That Goes Unpaid," the PBS NewsHour revealed in stunning detail the untallied dollar impact family caregiving has on our national economy. The actual dollar values reported were based on calculations by the Congressional Budget Office, an indication that the government, while perhaps not actively promoting the importance of family caregivers, is well aware of the incredible value they represent. As the report headlines, family caregiving would be a $234 billion dollar business if caregivers were paid just a paltry $11.16 per hour for their work in 2011 (the year for which the calculations were done). More revealing is the description of what that $234 billion represents in the context of the larger American economy. It actually moves the needle of the GDP (the country's gross national product), weighing in at 2 percent. As a federal agency, it would rank fifth largest, exceeded only by Health and Human Services, Social Security, Defense, and the Treasury. It would outrank the departments of Agriculture, Labor, and all other federal agencies. What's more, the "dollar value" of family care dwarfs the expenditures of every federal agency and private source involved in financing elder care. Compared to that $234 billion in annual family care value, Medicare paid out only $68 billion. Medicaid paid out just $60 billion. Private insurance contributed a miniscule $12 billion.

The discovery of these facts completely changed my view of my role as a family caregiver. Instead of viewing my duties and frustrations as individual burdens with no import or meaning beyond the limits of my personal experience, I came to understand my work as part of a large, unacknowledged, and vastly underappreciated contribution to our society, a quarter-trillion dollar in-kind gift to the nation. Family caregiving isn't just support to a dependent recipient or the impacted family, it is a support to the entire country. It isn't just kind, and generous, and the right thing to do. It is highly productive, strategically important, and even patriotic.

That's why I started being careful to distinguish between commercial caregiving services that are performed on-site in the home, and informal, unpaid, family-based caregivers. Commercial caregiving is an acknowledged enterprise, based on straight up fee-for-service transactions. The dollars generated by that work are captured in ordinary economic measures. Like other providers in the elder care universe, this impact is easily measured and valued as a social contribution. Not so with the work of family caregivers, which is a big reason I think family caregiving gets no respect. And it is a big part of the reason I think family caregivers tend to have a comparatively low opinion of themselves, their efforts, and their contributions, especially when compared to the well-employed professionals, paraprofessionals, and technical specialists with whom they regularly come into contact. It shouldn't be that way. And if we are ever going to close the circle, if we are going to achieve a real, functioning, and high-quality "continuum of care" in our health care system, it cannot continue to be that way.

- *Family Caregiver* — a family member, partner, friend, or neighbor who advocates for and provides on-going help or assistance to someone who is ill, disabled, or frail.

CHAPTER 5
All Kinds of Complications

One beautiful August morning in 2012 I came home from a trail walk to find my mother sprawled on the floor. Having driven to the trailhead, I had almost decided to go straight to the supermarket for a few groceries then on to some other shopping, but decided instead to go by home and scoop up Mom for a brief outing. My mom was then in her late eighties. Her health problems had become acute, leading to frequent emergency room visits and several hospitalizations. But I was still caring for her at home. Returning from my walk along a wooded, scenic trail, I felt refreshed and optimistic. That lasted until I opened the door to find Mom with her back against the couch, completely naked, legs crossed at the ankles, toes wriggling. At first I couldn't make sense of the scene. The house shoes she normally wore were across the room along with her gown and there were unidentified glistening puddles that looked suspicious. There was a curious expression on her face.

When I asked what had happened, she replied that she had fallen but didn't know how. She could only remember having taken a shower then stepping out of the bathroom intending to cross the living room to turn on a radio. Then she was on the floor. I rushed out of the house, popped the trunk, and sticking my head into the space to muffle the noise, I called the only person I could think of—my daughter. "She fell!" I wailed into the phone. After a brief conversation I turned and ran back into the house. There were no obvious injuries and Mom wasn't complaining of pain. I made a decision to get her dressed and into the car to transport her to a nearby urgent care clinic where we were frequent visitors and well known. If I had been thinking clearly I would not have attempted to move her, instead calling 911 and waiting for a response. But on this morning some other gear kicked in.

My mother was a trim and petite woman but as she aged, her weight became more concentrated around her midsection with other parts, especially her arms and legs becoming smaller and weaker. This made her awkward to handle. Grabbing a dining room chair while coaxing her to use whatever strength she could muster, I managed to get her off the floor and upright. The urgent care facility was just a few minutes away. From there she was transported by ambulance to the hospital to screen for a grand mal seizure or some other possible cause for her fall. As things worked out there was no evidence of permanent damage and by the time we left the hospital Mom was back to normal. I knew I had experienced something I did not want to happen again. Mom was clearly a fall risk. She had a walker and a medical alert necklace, but seldom remembered to use them. That was her stubbornness and perhaps a little vanity showing through. As the person mainly responsible for her well-being I had a decision to make. It was time for me to acknowledge that I was no longer able to care for my mother at home. As a fall risk she could not be left at home alone while I worked. It was time for me to start looking for a place where she could receive twenty-four-hour care and monitoring.

It didn't take long to figure out that putting Mom into an assisted living facility would cost big bucks—way more than I could afford to shell out. Although she had a small monthly income there were no other assets to tap. There were possible third-party sources of funding but they all required extremely detailed applications covering practically every aspect of a person's history and finances. To even begin thinking about pursuing these sources of funding I had to debrief Mom on a great deal of personal information I previously had no reason to inquire about. It was then that I discovered some things about my parents and our family's history that I didn't really want to know. I imagine this is an experience common to many family caregivers. The requirement to dig into the past, unearthing facts that are germane to establishing eligibility for some benefit or another can lead to astounding revelations, breathing new life into events that had been set aside, ignored, or pushed into some remote, unvisited corner of everyone's mind. Secrets.

By then my mother and father had not been a couple for nearly forty years. I was away at college when Dad left, so didn't know much about the collapse of the marriage. I did know that my mother had moved to California briefly in an attempt at reconciliation but apparently she was treated very badly, feeling stranded in an alien place with no friends or resources other that what my father was willing to provide. Finally she saved enough money to buy a bus ticket and escape back to our hometown in North Carolina.

To complete any of the applications required by agencies offering resources for assisted living, the first thing I had to do was establish the facts about Mom's marital status. I knew next to nothing about my father's property in California and how that might affect Mom's eligibility for various kinds of financial support. I was in possession of a document my father sent alleging savings and checking accounts, retirement accounts and insurance policies, including account numbers and contact information. It turned out my parents had never divorced; they were still after all this time, legally married. That meant I had to travel west to California and gather facts about my father that might be relevant to my mom's qualifications for assisted living. While there my brother and I met with a lawyer to establish definitively whether divorce documents had ever been filed.

But first a sidebar. There is a strong indication of genetically transmitted Alzheimer's disease on my father's side of the family. My paternal grandmother— his mother—died of complications of Alzheimer's. So when my brother and I flew out to California in March

2001 to investigate the status of my parents' marriage, it didn't come as too great a shock to learn that that we would be visiting with my father in a locked Alzheimer's facility. Further complicating this situation was the fact that people with whom my father associated during his time in California gradually, but legally, had assumed control of his affairs. Basically these people "owned" him. Stricken with advanced Alzheimer's dementia, my father had been declared incompetent and his person put under the control of these unrelated people. The only option open to my family would be for my brother and me to contest the arrangement by seeking to be appointed my father's legal guardians through a court challenge. The logistics and expenses associated with that made the idea impractical. During this trip I realized just how easy it can be for practically anyone to legally take over a vulnerable person's life if the proper safeguards are not in place. As it stood, although we were my father's children, my brother and I could not even take him out of the state. Recounting the details of this sad episode with my mother, I suggested that we sit down and work through her own finances and make arrangements that would protect her as she continued to age, as it was likely that her existing health ailments would become more severe. But she clammed up, refusing to discuss the matter.

Several years passed. Intermittently, I raised the issue of putting into place the paperwork that could protect my mother should her physical or mental condition reach the point that she couldn't manage her own affairs. Her resistance to the idea was consistent. Then, just prior to Mom's fourth hip replacement surgery in 2010, at the age of eighty-five, I took a different tack. I suggested that she reach out to my daughter, her granddaughter, to have a discussion about the essential documents people needed to have at an advanced age. My daughter had worked for years in the insurance industry, steadily moving up the ranks of corporate management. Mom was extremely proud of her and the success she enjoyed in her professional career. This approach gained traction. Eventually my daughter coached Mom through completion of a durable power of attorney, which was assigned to me, and a health care power of attorney, which was assigned to my brother. Then in a real surprise one morning my mother suggested we take a trip to the bank so that she could add my name to her account. Although she had mentioned this possibility a couple of times, I considered it "thinking out loud," and didn't push the issue. I figured when she was ready, she would do it. And that is exactly what happened. Finally I could breathe easier. We were now moving toward being reasonably well positioned to handle a health-related calamity if one were to unexpectedly occur.

These were timely developments. While Alzheimer's disease, affects a lot of people and gets lots of media coverage, Alzheimer's isn't the only form of dementia out there. Any kind of dementia can create big problems for the caregiver and not just in the sense that it makes caregiving more complicated. It can actually create big problems with obtaining legal authority to act on behalf of the care recipient. Shortly after Mom signed off on the various papers giving my brother and me authority to act on her behalf when she could not, I discovered that one of her doctors had entered into her medical record a diagnosis of vascular dementia. The key to one person giving another the authority to act on their behalf is that the person granting that power must be of sound mind. A demented person cannot legally convey such authority. It is not that my brother and I could not have managed to represent Mom after the diagnosis of dementia, but it could have been a lot more difficult and if controversy arose in the course of her care, subject to challenge.

This brings me back to the subject of electronic medical records. There was only one reason I knew that a diagnosis of vascular dementia had been made with respect to my mom's cognitive functions: I discovered the entry myself by rooting around in her electronic medical records. The diagnosis was made and entered into her record by Mom's primary care physician. Of course we spoke generally with the doctor about Mom's forgetfulness as well as her sensitivity to opioids. Interestingly, although I accompanied Mom to most appointments with this physician and had many such conversations about her health issues, nothing about his diagnosis of vascular dementia was ever mentioned to me or to my mother as far as I know. This is an example of why electronic medical records can be so important to family caregivers and the people they care for.

As soon as I became aware that online records were available in the care system we used, I encouraged Mom to sign up. Being fluent with computers and having my own long history of interactions with the medical industry as well as my own big, fat, medical file, I was able to help her immediately start navigating her data. We discovered among other things that we did not have to wait until our next appointment or a call from the doctor's office to get lab results. They were usually posted within 48 hours. We were able to see all her diagnoses, some doctors' notes, a complete inventory of medications, and upcoming appointments, as well as hospital summaries and test results over time. If we had not executed the legal documents granting financial and health care powers of attorney, the diagnosis of dementia could have derailed efforts to secure third-party financing for assisted living, for example. Attempting to get that authority after such a diagnosis would have been immeasurably more difficult. Without electronic medical records it may have been months or years before I learned of the entry. One thing I have discovered about the eldercare industry is this: knowing is better than not knowing.

Because so much attention is given to Alzheimer's, people automatically think of that disease when the word "dementia" is uttered. But, as I said, all dementia is not Alzheimer's. Mom had risk factors for vascular dementia including high blood pressure, atrial fibrillation, and the wear and tear of aging—all of which take a toll on the brain's blood vessels. Mom's dementia was caused primarily by congestive heart failure, hence the vascular part. Basically her heart was too weak to consistently pump a sufficient amount of oxygenated blood to her brain. Treatment focused on lowering her blood pressure, starting a blood thinner, and implanting a pacemaker. The actual manifestations of vascular dementia can be highly variable. Mom might be alert, exhibiting great awareness and memory at one time, then completely in a fog of confusion and forgetfulness at other times. Over the years she had many cognitive tests. I learned that her performance on such tests could be influenced by acute illness, depression, pain, fatigue, and medication. Her first cognitive screen missed being perfect by just three points. In just two years it had fallen seven points. After several hospitalizations, and corresponding periods of rehabilitation, it rebounded to just one point below her baseline. So it is important to know what kind of dementia has been diagnosed in a care recipient. There are many types other than Alzheimer's.

The patient's mental condition and fitness to make health-related decisions serves as a reminder that there are two sides to the care equation: the caregiver and the care recipient. The circumstances under which the two are brought together do not always allow for the kind of planning and anticipation of problems that would be possible under ideal circumstances. All too often caregivers are thrown into their roles by sudden, catastrophic events, or slip into the obligation through performing simple acts of kindness. Either way, they are usually unprepared for and overwhelmed by the rigors and sacrifice caregiving demands. The care recipient, the person for whom the sacrifices are being made, is typically focused on her own problems, and oblivious to the burden every request or assumption imposes on the person providing care. For example my mother had long been afflicted with osteoarthritis and had a third hip surgery in 1996. Her suffering under the pain of this condition was such that I welcomed the surgery without giving any thought to what its aftermath might bring. Although we were living in the same household the notion that her recovery from surgery might disrupt the established routines of our lives never crossed my mind. After the surgery and during recovery a hospitalist asked Mom, "Mrs. King, do you live alone?" She promptly and proudly declared that she lived with me, her daughter. In hindsight, this was unfortunate, as Mom never understood the real purpose of the question, which was to determine whether she needed to be referred to a rehabilitation facility for surgical recovery. In fact no one ever mentioned the possibility of her being discharged to a rehab facility. The doctor simply assumed that I, the daughter, would be at home and available to oversee Mom's rehabilitation and therapy.

Therefore, despite the fact that I worked a full-time job, Mom was discharged to home-based therapy.

Later I learned that following at least a 3-day hospital stay and circumstances that indicate patient debilitation, doctors routinely recommend and Medicare pays for institutional rehabilitation and therapy. Rehab is intended to bring the patient back up to baseline physical abilities in strength and dexterity. Hospitals even employ staff to find available rehab beds and make the necessary arrangements for admission. The question put to Mom by the hospitalist that morning and her impromptu response effectively canceled that option for us. Mom was assigned home-based therapy, but since she could not get up and open the door for the therapist, I had to leave work at midday to do that. Then I had to make up the time missed from work—meaning my workday stretched into the evening, disrupting meals and other routines. This was a lesson. Questions put to patients by medical personnel are asked for a reason. And here's the secret: you have to understand what is being asked and why. Questions are not necessarily phrased to encourage thoughtful consideration by the patient or the caregiver. Just because Mom did not have the presence of mind to say, "I live with my daughter but she works full-time," we got saddled with weeks of stressful and disruptive home-based rehabilitation that would have gone much more efficiently and smoothly in a local rehab facility.

CHAPTER 6
The Search

As I have said, every person takes a different path into the role of family caregiver. My path was gradual, so gradual I didn't even see it coming. Therefore I found myself knee deep in caregiving responsibilities without the slightest idea of how to prioritize or manage those responsibilities. To start almost everything was on a catch as catch can basis. Eventually, as the responsibilities settled in, becoming a permanent part of my daily life, certain routines and a problem solving capacity began to be established. That happened over the course of a lot of years. My learning curve could have been accelerated by the availability of educational support specific to the basic challenges faced by family caregivers. In particular training that addressed hands-on work such as interacting with the medical establishment, compliance with treatment protocols, dealing with various funding agencies, managing medications, assisting with physical tasks such as bathing, toileting, safe lifting and moving all would have been helpful. A primer on sensible, affordable ways to modify a house to reduce the risk of falls, or ways to identify side effects from medicines such as depression or sudden mood changes would also have been helpful.

Guidance on these subjects exists of course, but it is widely scattered and not targeted to family caregivers.

Most caregivers don't have time or energy to go searching for randomized information and then puzzle through how it all fits together. They are busy juggling responsibilities. So they just do the best they can, making it up as they go along. Although family caregivers are a huge and important component of the overall health care system, the last link in the "continuum of care," AARP caregiver surveys indicate the overwhelming majority of them actually receive no formal training. Much the same can be said about resources for identifying and vetting providers such as home health services, adult day care programs, and assisted living enterprises. The market is unfiltered. The family caregiver has but one piece of advice she can truly rely on: let the buyer beware.

During my caregiving tenure I always worked a full-time job. Most family caregivers work (sixty percent according to AARP). The schedule of "helping" services usually offered to family caregivers in my area struck me as especially odd. Nearly all the programs and other activities aimed at the elderly and their helpers were scheduled during business hours on weekdays. It seems that these programs were planned more for the convenience of the staffs than the people who were supposedly being served. For example, I attempted to keep my mother enrolled in a daycare program at a local senior center but it was just too difficult. Mom would have to be rousted from bed at six a.m. to have enough time to get her bathed and dressed, have breakfast, and take her medication, before I dropped her off at the center and peeled rubber to work for my eight a.m. start time. Everything was slow for my eighty-five year old care recipient. After four hip surgeries and crippling arthritis she was a fall risk and the walk from my front door to the street was full of steps and changing elevations, making getting her to and from van transit impractical. I had to back my SUV right up to the porch. My work day ended at five p.m., the same time the program terminated, but I had to navigate a cross-town trip through heavy, often halting or stalled traffic before arriving to pick her up. The staff was not pleased that Mom was always one of the last clients to leave the premises. Clearly this "service" was intended for caregivers able to accommodate a very limited, inflexible schedule.

Frequently I was referred to online resources, particularly AARP, which does have a wide range of accurate, easy to understand information useful to anyone concerned with eldercare issues. Most of the "training" I discovered through this and other websites was, once again, offered during weekday business hours. When I did find a local caregiver's conference or information session conveniently scheduled on a weekend or in the evening, I was offered "goodie bags" full of printed information and promotional materials. After a long day or week of caregiving it is easy for that information to slide right off your lap when you finally get a chance to sit down and relax. But I was most perplexed by what was missing from many of the sessions I did attend. Why weren't clinics or hospitals providing short "how to" sessions on using online portals for electronic health records? Where were the public and private transportation services designed to remove mobility barriers to healthcare access? Why weren't there breakout sessions or signups for hands-on help with those complicated applications for various kinds of financial assistance, even if offered on a fee-for-service basis? Why weren't there more product demonstrations or how-to videos? Frankly instead of leaving every seminar or conference with a goodie bag of paper, I would rather have had a door prize of one hour of respite care from a home health company.

The eldercare industry is a realm unto itself with its own vocabulary and terminology. Without much in the way of instruction or guidance I picked my way along, working diligently to understand the differences among various kinds of care arrangements or facilities—assisted living, family care home, personal care home, skilled nursing facility. It was all very confusing. What kind of facility would be the best match for my mother's condition at a given phase of her physical decline? I spent a lot of time online researching information presented on organization websites and much more time actually driving around visiting facilities.

To reduce my initial confusion I engaged an online company that was a fee-based broker. It made referrals to various types of service providers. However, I wasn't particularly happy with the recommendations being made. Eventually, after reading the fine print on the broker's website, I realized that the referrals made were all members of a limited network that covered only a small percentage of the many options for assisted care in the area. I found it is important to carefully read the fine print on *everything* having to do with eldercare.

After deciding to take matters into my own hands, I started looking for a place on my own, using recent online reviews posted by other caregivers who commented on their experiences with one or another care facility. Using this source I eventually found an assisted living facility for my mom. It seems to me that in this day and time, the kind of scattershot, random searching I did should be unnecessary. After all if I want to buy a product online, there are almost unlimited ways to screen and compare vendor offerings. But when it comes to serving our elderly population there are very few filters. That's sad.

Another thing that puzzles me is the inordinate amount of attention given to the psychological health of family caregivers as compared to a dearth of direct support and training that if provided could relieve much of that psychological distress. In my personal experience, what family caregivers need most are solutions—assistance with solving concrete problems that come with the role—not sympathy and handholding. So much of organized activity directed toward family caregivers is concerned with high levels of stress, mental fatigue, and physical exhaustion that plague the vast majority. All are of course important concerns, but it's as though no one stops to identify the exact causes of these complaints then gets busy on solutions that bring relief. Instead there is a proliferation of "group therapy" type sessions where people let off steam and enumerate grievances, then leave without any concrete tools to improve their lot. What these sessions amount to in my view is a few hours of satisfying emotional release, then an inevitable return to the same old same old. It brings to mind the old image of a dog chasing its tail.

In truth much of the information that proved valuable during my search for real guidance as a family caregiver came from hearsay. While sitting in the waiting area of an emergency room I might have a fruitful conversation with a stranger about Medicare experiences. It would be enough to send me googling the Medicare website for verification. A passing conversation with a nurse could yield tips about things to look out for with certain medications, including possible side effects that might not appear on the label.

Once when I was struggling to successfully complete an almost impossible application for Veterans Administration (VA) aid and attendance benefits, I scheduled a meeting with a VA field representative. I was desperate to identify funds that would allow me to afford a decent assisted living facility. The representative was not all that helpful with my VA application questions, but mumbled as if thinking out loud, "Your mother is probably eligible for Medicaid long-term care." I explained that Mom had already been declined for Medicaid because of income limits. He replied that the qualifications for long-term care and regular Medicaid were completely different, that they were two completely different programs. Of all the conversations I had with Mom's doctors, hospital administrators, social workers, various caregiver support personnel, and others about placing Mom in assisted care, no one had said anything about this. To make a long story short, I immediately and doggedly pursued this tip. After many months of a mind-numbing, bureaucratic, application process, and wrangling with local Medicaid administrators, I finally secured Medicaid long-term care funding to cover some of my mother's nursing care costs. So much of the information surrounding funding available from public agencies is hush-hush. If a person doesn't know or doesn't know to ask she is unlikely to be told. Like it is all a big secret.

Navigating the world of caregiving is time consuming and, if the caregiver is not careful to maintain a balanced perspective, it can be disruptive to a *normal* way of life. In fact, caregiving can become a way of life in and of itself. That is not healthy. It had to be brought to my attention that isolation is a real danger in the caregiving role. Helpful guidance can sometimes come from a wide range of casual encounters—the doctor's office, a chance conversation struck up at the grocery store, while waiting for the valet at the clinic, or chatting with other caregivers while entering or leaving the nursing facility. I had to learn to speak to and engage other caregivers.

I also learned that this "job" could produce infrequent but touching acknowledgements of one's special role as a caregiver—sometimes by complete strangers. A young man at a small family restaurant paid our breakfast tab long before I knew what was happening or I could thank him. A youngish woman having dinner with her spouse in a cafeteria-style restaurant swiped my bill from our table, paid it, and refused to accept anything more than a hug. It is important to graciously accept such acts of generosity, focusing on them instead of rude experiences such as people letting doors swing closed in the face of an obviously disabled person being assisted by a caregiver.

Of all my attempts at research and self-education none was more important than efforts to secure money to fund Mom's ongoing health related-expenses and long-term care. As Mom got older and her health continued to decline my personal financial burden increased substantially. Although covered by Medicare for hospitalizations, doctors' visits, and most prescription medicines, all these services required some cash expenditures in the form of deductibles or co-pays. Mother had a mind-boggling number of providers: a primary care physician; an orthopedic specialist; a cardiologist, an optometrist; an audiologist; a dentist; a pharmacist; and so on. Even though Medicare paid for or reimbursed for most physician approved needs, there were literally dozens of small, non-covered but necessary purchases that added up to real money over the course of a year: over-the-counter treatments for minor ailments; special pillows and bedding for comfort and safety; bath and toileting aids; custom shoe inserts and clothing; lotions and ointments; etc. While Mom had some limited regular income it was not nearly enough to cover all these out of pocket expenditures, not to mention the transportation expenses incurred while driving all over the region to keep appointments. The difference between what these obligations cost and what Mom could afford from her funds was made up by my income. By the time Mom fell for the first time and I realized her days of living with me were nearing an end, I had already started looking into possible sources of funding for financial relief and long-term care.

Several years into my stint as Mom's family caregiver I purchased a private long-term care insurance policy for myself. That decision grew from a realization that my chronic health issues would pose a real problem for me as I aged and the Crohn's disease I had struggled with nearly all my adult life was joined by other health problems that typically come with old age. The decision was probably motivated by the enormous amount of time I spent in hospitals, clinics, and doctors' offices, observing along the way enormous increases in the cost of medical treatment and constant changes in medical insurance coverage.

My medical record is not enviable, including two complete knee replacements, a bowel resection, and several other less drastic interventions. I take a fairly impressive list of medications, some of which are of the newfangled "biologic" variety. They are crazy expensive. With just one child to possibly call on for assistance during my own very likely debilitated old age, I felt that I needed an additional hedge against health-related calamity. But the clincher was fear that as an only child, my daughter's successful life of work and family could be upended by obligations to an aging, ill, dependent parent. In other words, I did not want to pass onto her the experience I was having as a family caregiver. One way to do that was to make an honest assessment of my situation, then take reasonable steps to minimize exposure and risk.

But my mother didn't have that opportunity. She came of age in a different time, a time of big, extended families and strong community bonds. There were twelve children in my mother's rural, farming family. In her era people mostly aged and died at home, cared for by relatives and a close knit community of friends and associates, often working through church ministries. Some of that still exists, but it is a vanishing scenario. Families are now much smaller, placing the burden of elder care on one or perhaps two children, if there are any children at all. And families are rarely as intact as they once were, with divorce, remarriage, and geographic mobility weakening the bonds that once provided the most reliable safety net. From my mother's cultural perspective, a long-term care insurance policy would have probably been so foreign as to not make any sense. But the assumptions on which her generation based its expectations about old age are now obsolete. All that is to say when it came to financing Mom's growing pile of medical bills as well as her inevitable commitment to some kind of assisted care facility, I found myself scrambling for answers—and for money.

My first effort to tap a public source offering financial assistance was Medicaid, the government program that serves the poor. Mom was subsisting on a low, fixed income, so I assumed she would qualify. Having Medicaid coverage to back her Medicare benefits would eliminate a lot of the out-of-pocket medical expenses that were eating up my disposable income. But there is a big difference between Medicare and Medicaid. A person who qualifies for Social Security is automatically enrolled in Medicare when she turns sixty-five. Payroll deductions made to the program during working years make automatic enrollment possible. Mom had the required work credits and had stepped into Medicare with no problem. But Medicaid is means tested, meaning a person has to qualify for the program based on income. Although low in my estimation, Mom's paltry Social Security and pension checks combined to put her less than fifty dollars above the cut-off for Medicaid approval. I was both surprised and deflated.

Mom's big fall was a kind of watershed event; her health took a marked turn for the worse after that. I was paranoid about her being at home alone, and for a while I was able to engage an agency that supplied an in-home aide to monitor and provide companionship to Mom during the day while I worked. At a rate of about $25 per hour this situation worked out for a while but there were coordination and logistical issues.

Meanwhile I was frantically searching for any possible source of funds that would relieve the cash drain on my checkbook or provide money to enable Mom to enter an assisted living arrangement. At some point, I received a referral to a retired military officer whom I was told could assist me in applying for Veterans Administration benefits.

In the course of investigating my father's background, I discovered that he had served in a combat role in the army during WWII. There appeared to be a special survivor's benefit available to widows of those veterans. The referral was a good one, but the officer was swamped with requests for assistance.

Eventually she got back to me. We had a conversation about my mom and my dad's service record. Her assessment was that Mom could indeed be qualified for a VA benefit providing aid and attendance to combat veterans. But she was completely covered up with work and would be unable to get to my case for some time. She warned that the application was difficult, labor intensive, and that the process of evaluation would take a considerable period of time. Most people, she said, undertook the process with the assistance of a lawyer. From the information gleaned during our phone conversation, I convinced myself that I could complete the application successfully without a lawyer. So I set about doing just that.

The VA application was everything the officer said it would be. Extremely detailed, it forced me to retrace much of the family and career histories I had been doing on my mother and father. Only the VA wanted a much deeper examination of the facts and actual copies of all relevant documents. So I found myself researching, identifying, copying, and sorting a veritable mountain of forms, certificates, records, discharges, and all manner of other service-related materials. It was necessary to double check and verify dates and timelines since they were not all obvious or consistent. This required many hours of painstaking attention to the tiniest of detail and fanatical concentration. Much of this work was performed late at night, on my bed, computer aglow, paper spread out everywhere. On many nights I dozed off with the laptop at my side, it springing to life whenever jolted out of silent mode by my troubled sleep.

The extraordinary detail and physical documentation demanded by the VA application was not even its most intimidating feature. That honor went to the phrasing of the questions, which was for lack of a better word, "tricky." The wording of some of the questions was so vague or odd it left me bewildered as to just what response was being sought. And, there seemed to be a lot of repetition. The same basic question asked several different ways—like a test of consistency. I called VA help lines many times requesting clarification but with little satisfaction.

Finally, I figured I was just on my own. So I hunkered down, put myself in the place of the VA as guardian of a huge bag of money that people were trying to dip into. That strategy guided me throughout the aid and attendance application process. It helped greatly that sometime prior, on a whim, I had taken a paralegal course at a local university. I didn't want to be a lawyer and didn't want to work as a paralegal. I did want the ability to think critically within rule-based systems—which is how I view the law—and develop skills in the kind of deductive reasoning that makes those systems work. Paralegal training was great preparation for dealing with all the bureaucratic organizations—the VA, Medicare, Medicaid, hospitals, etc.—with which I constantly wrestled as a family caregiver.

The officer's warning about a long, drawn out evaluation period was also on point. After completing the application—being sure to keep a complete copy of the entire document for my records—the real period of frustration began. Every conceivable excuse for delaying a decision on approval was offered up by VA personnel. I was confident that the aid and attendance application I submitted was complete and of high quality. While I did not expect quick action on the package, I did not expect it to take weeks before the VA even acknowledged receipt. After that it was one thing after another. For example they would claim that I had not included or they "couldn't find" some document or another. This happened repeatedly. Since I had a complete copy of the submitted package I knew that was false. At any rate I could offer to immediately email or fax another copy. Usually that prompted them to "find" the original. Sometimes I would simply tell the representative to thumb through the package to a certain page number. "Oh, there it is," they would say.

Weeks led to months. I was calling and checking on the status of the application several times a week, pushing the organization to act, but trying to be nice, trying not to alienate the employees who I understood were just doing their jobs. I was complaining about the delays to a friend one day and he said, "If she dies, they don't have to pay anything. They are delaying because they know that of the people who have been approved, a bunch of them will die waiting to be paid." I hadn't thought of that. This was a survivor's benefit payable only to the surviving spouse. If Mom died, the VA was off the hook for a fair amount of money.

Finally I managed to schedule a meeting with a VA official to discuss why my mom's application was taking so long to be approved. We discussed the package I had submitted. He was impressed with its thoroughness and asked who helped me put it together. Nobody I said; I had done it myself. His brow wrinkled in mild disbelief. "We rarely get an applicant who is able to do this without assistance. Most people retain a lawyer or VA representative."

Not long after that meeting I was notified that the application had been approved, and the amount of the monthly benefit Mom was entitled to. The monthly payments would start fairly soon, but she would also be due a lump sum of back pay from the date the application was submitted. The application had been in process for many months, so the lump sum payment would be substantial. That was important because we had already made an arrangement, negotiating a deal to move Mom into an assisted living facility that agreed to defer a portion of the monthly fee so that we could handle the payments from our family resources. The unpaid portion would accumulate and be carried until the VA back pay was received. It would then be paid off in a lump sum.

This was a risky arrangement. The unpaid portion of the monthly fee quickly amounted to thousands of dollars. The portion we were able to cover along with other related expenses was putting a huge strain on my household budget. I felt enormous pressure to get that VA back pay. So I started calling and calling and the VA just delayed and delayed. It was in process, coming anytime now, probably just a few weeks away. The promises were endless. But no check came.

Meanwhile I was growing frustrated with the assisted living facility—actually a family care home—and wanted to move Mom to a place offering skilled nursing services, but the overhang of deferred, unpaid fees prevented that. My independent, self-directed search for information and resources had been successful in many ways, but I was still facing quandaries and dilemmas. It was like peeling an onion. There were layers of challenges and frustrations. But I was making progress, and that was enough to keep me motivated. It is of vital importance that family caregivers understand the differences that categorize various kinds of nursing and assisted living facilities so that a correct choice can be made when matching a loved one's needs to an institution's licensed services and capabilities:

- Personal care home (PCH) – Residences that provide housing, meal service with supervision, and assistance with personal care tasks for two or more adults who are unable to care for themselves but do not need nursing home or medical care. Inspected and licensed. Usually privately owned, although may be operated by local governments or nonprofit agencies.

- Family care home (FCH) – A private residence licensed to provide housing, meals and personal care services to older and disabled adults who are unable to live independently. Intended to be a less costly alternative to institutional settings for individuals who do not need twenty-four-hour nursing supervision. Usually two to six beds.

- Assisted living facility — Housing for people with disabilities or adults who cannot or choose not to live independently. Similar to a retirement home in that it provides a group living environment and typically caters to an elderly population. Regulated and licensed at the state level. Some assisted living facilities are called personal care homes. The size can vary from a few to hundreds of residents. Residents usually need assistance with at least one of the activities of daily living (ADLs).

- Rehabilitation center — A facility providing physical therapy or any other treatment designed to restore "baseline" capacities after an illness, surgery, hospitalization, or trauma involving loss of function. Patients are evaluated to determine the extent of their debilitation, a regimen of appropriate therapy, and their ability to participate in treatment.

- Nursing home — Private institution providing a place of residence for people who require continual nursing care and have significant difficulty coping with the required activities of daily living. May also be referred to as a convalescent/rest home, long-term care or skilled nursing facility.

CHAPTER 7
Making it Work

During the entire period that my mother lived with me I was employed full-time. There were also periods when I worked an additional part-time job. Those ranged from coffee shops, to emergency room registration, to temporary survey research assignments. There was even one evening gig at a car dealership. My primary employment was at a private secondary school where I had responsibilities consisting mainly of collecting, crediting, and tracking donations. It was a job that required attention to detail. During busy periods, such as the end of the year when charitable donations poured in, the hours could be long and the pressure to complete transactions could be unnerving. As a person with Crohn's disease, which is exacerbated by stress, this may not have been an ideal situation, but the pay was adequate, and the overall work environment pleasant. Most of all, in due course I was able to work out an arrangement for flexibility.

Through survey research AARP has found that most caregivers work and fifty-six percent of them work full-time. According to AARP the demands of caregiving often require changes in employment or work situations such as cutting back on hours, taking leaves of absence, or receiving demerits due to repeated absences and tardiness. The more hours spent on caregiving activities, the more likely these things happened. Caring for a close relative or spouse demanded the highest number of hours and so a caregiver in that situation would normally be subject to the greatest workplace pressure. Unlike most developed countries, the U.S. doesn't have any kind of comprehensive family leave policy, so each working caregiver is on her own, trying to solve the workplace problem in isolation and without much in the way of societal support.

I have been working on my job for more than twenty years. In many ways I am surprised to be still on the payroll. During the craziest periods of caregiving as well as attending to my own medical issues, I could be out for at least part of a day several days a month. Mom especially had many medical appointments and fairly regular medical emergencies. I had very little help in transporting her to appointments, and at any rate as her patient advocate, needed to be present most times so my knowledge of her various medical conditions remained up to date.

As the absences continued I worried more and more about job security. One day I mentioned this concern to Mom's geriatrician. She immediately offered to provide the required third party certification for Family and Medical Leave by describing Mom's medical diagnoses and the level of care needed to support the request. The Family Medical Leave Act (FMLA) is a federal law that took effect in 1993 to help balance workplace demands with the medical needs of employees and their families.

The law provides for twelve weeks of leave during a twelve-month period to care for an immediate family member with a serious health condition. An employee is required to substitute/use paid leave (sick, vacation, or personal days) during FMLA leave. Also the law applies to companies with fifty or more employees. Further, it is important to check fine print with the human resources department and the state labor law language.

The FMLA proposal did not go over particularly well when originally presented to my employer. Having been a supervisor with another employer I knew that the frequent absences and partial workdays were not acceptable. Although I would come in after hours and work weekends to keep current with my workload, I also understood that in a work environment appearances mean something. It seemed that my coworkers were getting the impression that I was someone who did not value her job. Feeling tremendous anxiety, the only thing that made me feel somewhat better was working hard and being productive whenever I was at my desk. That was the only thing I could really control.

In an attempt to demonstrate responsibility and accountability I made extraordinary efforts to communicate with my immediate supervisor. It is always important to keep the person to whom you report fully informed. That person has to be able to speak to the reason for your absence or other non-conforming workplace behavior. In an office environment there is also a kind of culture. There are things you do and things you don't do. You don't for example show up late for staff meetings. There were times when I did not plop down on my chair until fifteen minutes after a staff meeting had begun, sweating from embarrassment and full of anxiety. My supervisor and I had several uncomfortable conversations. My behavior was subject to formal evaluation and annual assessments. I often felt alienated, disconnected from office life. But the health care system was too complex and confusing for my mother to navigate alone, and most of the medical profession's business is conducted during working hours. I chose to support my mother although it was threatening my livelihood and sole source of income. So I just tried to keep my chin up, work my butt off, and refuse to make excuses.

The greatest single threat to job performance that I experienced as a caregiver resulted from sleep deprivation. This started in 1994 prior to mom's third hip surgery. She complained about pain throughout the night, frequently calling out and waking me from a sound sleep. As obvious as it appears in hindsight, I did not at the time make the connection between her pain, which elevated her blood pressure, high levels of medication, and the disintegrating quality of our nights.

While I was getting practically no sleep and feeling stymied at work, Mom was drowsy all day, medicated to the max in an effort to relax and control her blood pressure. Not only was she taking several blood pressure medications, but also a prescription med to relieve anxiety. At some point she got a narcotic added to fend off pain from degenerative joint disease. The mix of these meds put her in a near catatonic state much of the time while I struggled to keep my eyes open during the day.

After a while, it became impossible for me to sleep for more than a couple of hours at a time, always alert at night for sounds of discomfort from my mother's room. This situation went on for years. At one point I was referred for a sleep study. After getting all wired and prepped to be monitored, the researcher finally had to call off the session—I just couldn't go to sleep.

When Mom first moved in with me she had her own car and was fairly independent. As I've mentioned before, it was an old car and required frequent repairs. At some point a couple of years or so down the line, it became more trouble than it was worth. She got rid of it. Once she was without transportation, I became her taxi service. I left work at inconvenient times to pick her up from home, take her to appointments, wait for lab work, take her back home, and then return to work. My anxiety over the time I was missing from work was so great I could barely sit in a chair in waiting rooms, my leg bouncing up and down with nervous energy.

Although I imagine things will change in time as the demographics of this country make more people caregivers of older relatives, right now being absent from work to care for a dependent adult is regarded somewhat differently from absences related to say, a dependent child. Whereas reports of a sick child are met with genuine concern and even alarm, custodial care of an adult relative often meets with a somewhat less sympathetic reaction. So sometimes instead of attributing an absence to my mom's health issues, I would just say that I had a doctor's appointment (and I did have quite a few).

On good days I raced about town from one appointment to another playing beat the clock with uncooperative traffic. On bad days I contemplated throwing my hands up and ditching everything, having no idea how I would manage, but desperate for some kind—any kind—of relief.

Eventually the toll of caregiving plus the strain of office tension was just too much, forcing me to schedule a meeting with the head of the school where I worked. I went in with the idea of taking some time away from work to try to get my situation straightened out so that at some point I might be able to return and perform as expected. After listening to what I proposed, he countered with an idea I did not anticipate: an offer to work a different, flexible schedule.

That was the turning point. Having the option to adjust my work schedule to accommodate the most demanding caregiving duties while still executing work responsibilities made all the difference in my being able to hold on to my job. It was a job I needed and one that I performed well. I did not want to lose it. Now I didn't have to.

The bottom line is mixing caregiving and full-time employment is difficult but there are ways to make it work. As a somewhat reticent and private person, I have had to overcome a reluctance to discuss family matters in the workplace. There is a line separating honesty from over-sharing. The caregiver has to learn where and how to draw that line. There are non-verbal ways of expressing gratitude for being allowed to operate outside normal workplace hours. The willingness to come in after hours or to work on weekends so that normal office workflow is maintained goes a long way toward sustaining cordial relations. I learned to push the envelope when scheduling appointments—insisting on times that allow consolidation within a bracketed period on a given day to reduce the net amount of time taken away from work. I make a point to always acknowledge the help of office associates whose cooperation and support have bailed me out of many testy little situations. And I never fail to say thank you for any consideration granted in applying the flexibility I have been so fortunate to obtain because I realize the circumstances could very well be different.

These are some rules I created for myself to help manage the demands and complexities of working full-time while also operating as a primary caregiver:

- Resist the urge to over-share details of your caregiving experience in the workplace no matter how much empathy is shown. Provide information to those who have a need to know.

- Practice kindness toward yourself and coworkers. Make a concerted effort not to carry the stress of caregiving in your body language or on your countenance while at work.

- Know your company policies. Many companies allow employees to use sick leave not only for themselves but immediate family, including parents.

- Try to minimize adverse impacts on your job as well as relieve caregiver/recipient stress by consolidating appointments where feasible and allowing for extra travel time or possible delays. Having the presence of mind to do this reduces the likelihood of having two very unhappy and exhausted individuals at the end of the day.

- Look ahead for favorable scheduling opportunities. Target for appointments those days when your employer is closed but the doctor's office or clinic is open. Ask to be put on a waitlist or cancellation notification if your preferred days and times are booked.

- Make every effort to head off emergencies but when they occur, have an urgent care facility or similar provider identified that can provide treatment until the regular medical provider is available.

- Avoid unnecessary frustration by allowing twice as much time as you think may be required to prepare for an appointment or other activities taking into consideration dressing, transit, parking, registration lines, bathroom breaks.
- Always have small bottles of water along and prepackaged snacks to deal with wait times and delays. These also aid trip efficiency since having to make an extra stop for food or drink on days when you must return to work is usually not the best plan. Of course, a more leisurely pace is possible when you've taken the day off from work.
- Shop online for clothing and other necessities where possible, or to minimize frustration take a vacation day on a Monday to do your shopping or shop early on a Sunday twice a year.

CHAPTER 8
The Personal Care Home

After Mom's big fall it seems that things came to a head. Most importantly, the fall and its aftermath jarred my thinking into a sharp sense of reality. Mother could no longer safely stay in the home she had shared with me for over twenty years. It was at once a sad and frightening realization. Up to now my story has mainly revolved around the challenges and problems I encountered as a family caregiver. Despite all the frustrations and sacrifices that caregiving demanded, the thought of Mom leaving the household made me realize how much I had come to value her companionship. I must admit there were many more good times than bad ones. The realization that Mom would—at some point in the near future—not be around, made memories of those good times more precious. I began to recall them frequently and with deeper appreciation.

For example, Mom was very much a family person. During big holidays my small bungalow could have thirty people drop by for dinner, eating at card tables, sitting with plates in their laps on folding chairs, sofas and arm chairs. If the weather was nice, they would even sit out on the front porch, basking in the full sun offered by its southern exposure, even when the air was a little nippy. We would cook huge amounts of food, not just because everybody had big appetites, but because they would want to "fix a plate" of turkey, ham, potato salad, greens, mac-and-cheese, and dessert to take home. There was always boisterous fun at these affairs—old tales and family legends being told for the umpteenth time, each time further enriched by the imagination of the teller. Mom was the center of it all.

We also enjoyed getting all dolled up for church, helping each other with hair (back when I had some), fittings—"Can you zip me up?"—and makeup. These shoes? That necklace? Does this make me look big?

Although I came to harbor some resentment at the cavalier way she would urge me to buy things I really could not afford, Mom was a sharp dresser and a joy to shop with, even after she was in bad physical shape and relied on a walker. Other than going to church on Sunday mornings, her favorite outing was to the mall. We did a lot of window shopping of course, just oohing and aahing at this or that well-tailored garment, and especially at dazzlingly beautiful but impossibly expensive jewelry and shoes. It was great fun. We enjoyed trying on outfits for each to critique.

One incident in particular is indelibly etched into my memory. While in the dressing room of a well-known mid-range department store I thought I detected an odor, and then dismissed it as an unfortunate release of gas. As she got deep into her years Mom was known to do that...wherever. Unapologetic, she would say "More space out there than there is in me..." But this day was different. The odor did not dissipate. "Mom, are you

OK?" I asked. She said that she was, but I was suspicious. "Let's take a trip to the ladies room," I said. So we did. What I found was that my mom was not only incontinent, but I realized she had lost most of the sensation associated with the movement of her bowels. She wasn't even aware that she had soiled her adult diaper.

After a furious few minutes of cleaning and washing, all was well and we emerged from the powder room two refreshed ladies ready to resume our shopping. She looked at me, I looked at her, and we both burst out laughing like naughty schoolgirls. After that I never took Mom anywhere without extra adult diapers—in the car, in my purse, in the small compartment of her walker or wheelchair. Once bitten, twice shy.

Mom had enjoyed a very comfortable situation at my home. A small, three-bedroom bungalow in a cul-de-sac neighborhood that had a number of other elderly residents, it was a cozy set-up for her. I had made many changes over the years to make living with me relatively safe and convenient, including having a wheelchair ramp built, moving food and supplies to lower levels where she could easily access them, adding hardware to allow ease of use of bathing and toilet facilities, etc.

In choosing her next living situation I wanted to be as conscientious as possible. I made a list of the assistance Mom would need—meals, medication management, and assistance getting up from low seating, and transportation to appointments. I wanted a place that offered a continuum of care corresponding to phases of a resident's advancing needs, but quickly discovered I could not afford that. I wanted rocking chairs, fresh flowers, and low sodium meals prepared with fresh ingredients, activities, outings, a caring staff, and a safe, pleasant environment. Cost was of prime importance because Mom would be private pay. She could not qualify for Medicaid, had received nothing from my father or his estate. Mom had no savings and of course, no long-term care insurance coverage. We could not afford much of anything on my wish list. My research and visits to personal care homes made me aware of a couple of things. First, it is difficult if not impossible to discover on the basis of a cursory visit, what is really provided in such a home; and second, that the fees charged by these facilities are not standardized. Many of the places I visited left me with an unsettled feeling, giving the impression that I would want to check in frequently to see that my mom was doing OK. They did not outwardly appear dangerous or badly run, but I had a feeling that things would be better if I were close by than far away. So I decided to focus my efforts on finding a facility close to my home and one with a home-like feel, which I felt would be in keeping with my mom's preferences and expectations.

I will be the first to admit that my mother was "spoiled" by the attentions and care I afforded her. Mom had always been particular about her personal appearance and hygiene, as well as the cleanliness and appearance of her overall living environment. She imparted many of those same standards and expectations to me. While we lived together Mom was comfortable and satisfied. But I knew it would be difficult to reproduce those conditions in any commercially operated assisted living situation, except at the most exclusive level, which we could not afford. So I decided to do the best I could, and thought I found the best candidate in a "family care home" located just a couple of miles from my residence. The house, a rambling one story ranch in a settled neighborhood, looked like a large single-family residence, which it had been for most of its existence. Now it provided shelter and daily assistance to a small group of eighty-somethings.

In my state, North Carolina, family care homes can take in up to six people in a family-type setting, providing around the clock support and monitoring by live-in staff who prepare meals, supervise medications, and provide help with dressing and other needs. The six-person limit is intended to ensure that family care homes meet zoning regulations that limit the number of unrelated people who can share a residential dwelling. The family-like setting means basically that residents share meals, common areas, furnishings, and other amenities much like members of a regular family. Family care homes are licensed and regulated by county and state officials. They must meet fire and safety requirements, and dietary standards—including posting and adhering to a daily menu. They also usually provide transportation to and from medical appointments and have formally scheduled activities for residents. The homes are owned privately and supervised by a manager who is certified for the job by passing a test administered by the county. The state and county, as licensing agencies, are also responsible for periodic inspections of the premises to ensure regulatory compliance or for responding to complaints about violations and abuse.

As described earlier, my brother and I arranged with the owner to pay the biggest portion, but not all of the monthly fee, allowing the difference to accumulate pending receipt of a lump-sum back payment of benefits we expected to receive from the Veterans Administration. The arrangement, which was based primarily on Mom's income from Social Security and her small pension, covered room and board and transportation. I paid medication costs above what was covered by Medicare Part D. This varied from $50 to $175 per month. Other than some modest family support, I basically covered all other costs such as bedding, towels and washcloths; television, radio, clothing, and toiletries. I also provided a cell phone, a fan, weight scale, walker, nebulizer, and even pillows to raise the height of chars, making it easier for Mom to get up and down for seating. The upside of this arrangement was that I could outfit Mom's room and provide her with personal items of a quality to which she was accustomed. The downside was that this turned out to be a fortunate coincidence because the owner reinvested little back into the business. Within a month of moving in, Mom complained of back pain during the night. Upon inspecting her bed I found the mattress and box spring to be completely worn out. Pointing out their condition to the owner, he promised replacements. After a week or so and no replacements arrived, I simply moved Mom's entire bed from my home into her room.

Observing the manner in which laundry was handled at the family care home caused me to decide that it would be advisable to continue doing Mom's laundry at home. That way I could be sure that the various types of fabric and colors would be properly sorted, cleanly washed, and neatly folded and/or ironed. Since the location was near my home and basically on my route to and from work, this was pretty easy to do. It should have been unnecessary.

Over the years I met a handful of really capable and dedicated people working as staff in elder care facilities, but in general employees are poorly paid. They often present well for family and visitors, but once the spotlight is turned off, backslide to a much less attentive and responsible work style. My mom regularly reported as much, and it showed up in numerous ways. There is a lot of turnover, and even the professional or technical people brought in on contract can leave a lot to be desired. Once, after one of her numerous hospitalizations, I was waiting with my mother in her room for a registered nurse to come by and do a follow-up examination. When the nurse entered the building she immediately came to Mom's bedside and started to unpack her valise to begin the assessment. I noticed her hands right away. Each of her nails had a visible line of dirt beneath them. When I objected to her conducting any procedure or even touching my mother without first thoroughly washing her hands, she was offended. Oh, but I was offended more. What medical professional does not automatically follow the protocol of hand washing (or at least pulling on a pair of gloves) before engaging in patient contact? She washed her hands, and I made sure that medical service provider was never sent to my mother again.

Issues related to diet arose again and again. Although a weekly menu was composed and posted at the home, it was rarely followed, compliance depending largely on who happened to be working. Mom had contracted high blood pressure during the birth of my younger brother who was then over fifty years old, so she had been burdened with the ailment for a very long time. Except for tomatoes I rarely used canned vegetables and avoided other sodium rich foods because her salt intake had to be strictly controlled. The home was aware of this. Yet they frequently served high-sodium foods such as canned soups, vegetables, and processed meats. When I mentioned my concern to the staff I was told they "rinsed" the canned foods to remove the salt. I started making healthy, homemade soup, freezing portions, and delivering them to Mom regularly.

Another interesting aspect of this particular elder care enterprise was although they were supposedly regulated by at least two government agencies, they flouted the regulations openly—only bringing things ship shape when inspectors were scheduled to visit. They seemed to have some idea when inspectors were coming. I would go by and everything would be orderly with all surfaces gleaming.

There were issues with transportation, as a vehicle was not always operating or was just not available to take Mom to appointments and I would have to leave work to take her. And there were too many "bird baths" for my mom's taste. She preferred a full shower every day, and for whatever reason, a wash-up in the sink was all she was given on many occasions.

Mom stayed in the family care home for about two years. She seemed mostly comfortable but also on edge. Then she began to experience complications of congestive heart failure. The heightened symptoms landed her in the hospital for three days at the end of 2014, ten days in January 2015, and several days the following month. From there she was discharged to a rehabilitation facility for physical therapy.

Upon being discharged she would need constant skilled nursing care, which the family care home could not provide. While she was at the family care home I had to keep an eye on Mom's physical condition—

frequently checking her feet, legs, abdomen and face for signs of fluid retention. Over time I watched while she lost interest in activities, became increasingly sluggish, and napped frequently, especially after meals. Thus began my adventures with Medicare paid rehab, requiring identification of a twenty-four-hour nursing facility, which prompted a side trip to Medicaid long-term care. It was an odd, surreal, and in many ways, terrifying journey. There are many potential problems and risks that come with entrusting a loved one to the care of institutions and commercial service providers. These are some things I learned to pay special attention to:

- Complaints by residents of facilities may sometimes be related to the care environment or staff performance and not necessarily to physical ailments, so observe and listen closely.

- Visit at random times. Check out the posted menu and ensure that meals being served are comparable to what is posted. It's reasonable to want to know how the food tastes.

- While the prevailing attitude is that elderly patients are not active enough to need a daily shower, ensuring that the care recipient enjoys good hygiene with frequent showers minimizes the risk of a wide range of infections. Monitor fluid intake and encourage the care recipient to use the bathroom several times a day.

CHAPTER 9
On Hospitals and Such

It is hard to remember the first time I encountered the term "hospitalist." It could not have been more than a couple of years ago. At first I was puzzled. The term was so awkward—so weird—it made me wonder what job a person saddled with such a label could possibly be charged with doing. So it was quite surprising when I found out that "hospitalist" was just another name for "doctor." It designates a certain kind of doctor, one who instead of hanging out a shingle and offering services from a private practice, instead chooses to be employed by a hospital. Hospitalists are usually drawn from among primary care specialties such as internal medicine and pediatrics. As I began to grasp the meaning of the word, "hospitalist," I began to better understand the subtle, but large-scale, transformative reorganization taking place in our health care delivery system. The word symbolized many small and large shifts I had witnessed during more than thirty years of intensive interaction with medical institutions and providers. In my view that one word capped an evolution that went from small, private medical practices, to big networks, and finally to a more corporate form of medical administration and management. It gave me a sense of where access to medical services might be going in the future, and what that could mean for me as: (1) a large volume consumer of medical services; and (2) caregiver and advocate for another person who also consumes a large volume of medical services.

To be clear, my own experience with the medical industry has generally been good. It has been my great fortune to be employed mainly by large institutions and organizations that offered excellent private health plans readily accepted by health care providers. In addition, I have lived in areas with top-notch medical infrastructure, including big research hospitals affiliated with prominent state-funded and private universities. As such I have generally had access to well-trained medical personnel, and the latest in medical technologies. I have even had the opportunity to participate in some clinical trials and experimental therapies. In other words, I have for the most part had access to the best that the system has to offer to more or less ordinary working people. And even with this level of expert medical attention there have been mishaps, some of them severe. There have been questionable surgeries, damaging drug therapies, and a fair share of doctor/patient conflicts. Personal experience as both patient and caregiver has taught me that even under best-case scenarios for medical access and treatment, total patient/caregiver engagement in health care decision-making is the best guarantee of successful outcomes. Getting there is the challenge.

Whatever the organizational form—private practice, network, corporate system—patients and caregivers have important responsibilities in health maintenance and wellbeing. That said, patients and caregivers must be given the tools and training to make the substantial contributions to health care goals that they are capable of making. The failure of the system to do this is clearly reflected in the finding by AARP that although nearly sixty percent of family caregivers perform critical medical/nursing tasks, only fourteen percent report receiving any instruction or training in performing those tasks. This could account in large measure for repeat hospitalizations that are driving up health costs and creating management headaches for healthcare institutions. In my mother's case I administered serious medicines for years—including barbiturates, opioids, diuretics, and blood thinners—with incomplete understanding of their potential interactions. As a person with a long history of intensive medical treatment herself, plus a lot of self-education, I was in a much better position to wrap my mind around these things than someone with little or no background. Yet I often found myself in a quandary. It seems to make sense, especially in an era of cost cutting and efforts to reduce readmissions that caregivers to patients discharged after serious hospitalizations should be offered basic instructions and support for proper care as well as compliance with protocols appropriate to a patient's case. This seems a no-brainer for reducing subsequent emergencies and readmissions, and avoiding unnecessary costs.

As mentioned in Chapter 2, electronic medical records represent a great advance insofar as providing instantly available information about a patient's medical history and current condition. Getting patients and caregivers up to speed on mastering the online platform as well as interpreting data in the files should be seen as a job someone has to do. I was in a position to train myself in this particular task, and very likely most of Gen X and the Millennials will be up to speed with the digital technology. But there are ten thousand people being added to the sixty-five and older cohort *every day* who may not be up to speed, and these are the people whose health care costs threaten to bankrupt the medical system in coming decades. Also medical records, electronic or not, cannot substitute for doctor/patient transparency. In my mother's case, the availability of online records helped me discover a doctor's unshared diagnosis of vascular dementia, but it would have been much more helpful for the doctor to have disclosed that diagnosis to us during the many occasions we were in his office receiving treatment and counsel.

The shift to a centralized, top-down, corporate type medical system, especially in hospitals and large medical institutions, but also nursing homes and rehab centers, has made me much more wary of a potential divergence between patient care and business objectives. Like most people, I am stunned by the incredible escalation of medical costs in this country and think we all have a role in reining in those costs. However, when a decision is made regarding my or my mom's health status or care plan, I want to be sure that decision is based on medical criteria, not a business plan.

Health decisions should be grounded in a medical evaluation, not a business analysis. This concern was brought into focus by a series of medical emergencies following a previous hospital stay, during which Mom was confined to the hospital and treated, but not formally admitted as a patient. She was placed in a "holding area" for "observation" instead of being formally admitted although her condition would have ordinarily resulted in admission.

The problem, it turned out, was that since she had been admitted to the hospital for an extended stay a few weeks earlier, a readmission would have adversely affected the hospital's performance statistics as judged by Medicare and other third party payment systems. These performance statistics, which were being protected by my mother's confinement in a kind of medical limbo, impacted the hospital's bottom line.

At first I was mystified as to why Mom was not being formally admitted to the hospital for care, but once the business aspect of the arrangement became clear there was no mystery at all. The hospital had a disincentive to readmit patients who had recently been discharged. So it created a different residential category, a "non-admission" in-treatment status called "observation."

These are the kinds of management maneuvers a patient and caregiver must be aware of to understand shifting strategies about treatment and underlying motives, to ensure appropriate accountability and make informed decisions that are in the best interest of the person being treated.

One of the caregiver's primary responsibilities is to ensure that medical providers help or that at the very least they do no harm. An incident that occurred in 2010 made me wonder why well trained physicians choose to interrogate elderly, heavily medicated patients about their conditions even in the presence of an advocate, when it is clear that the patient is confused or impaired.

After wrestling to stabilize her blood pressure for several weeks, my mother was referred to a specialist. Following a rather brusque greeting, the doctor asked my mother why she had come to see him. His tone was not friendly. Then he started rapidly asking questions without even looking at her. As her advocate I inquired whether he had not received information about her case from the referring physician. He ignored my question and proceeded to ask my mother about her blood pressure readings, which we had dutifully recorded. When she tried to hand him the sheet of recorded readings, he snapped that she could hold onto it until he finished his review. Then he continued in rapid-fire fashion to question the various bottles of medication she had brought along without fully giving her the opportunity to explain that the medications and doses had been changed many times in an effort to find an effective combination. Mom tried to explain that for many weeks she had been awakened between three and five a.m. with ringing in her ears, a burning sensation in her legs, back pain, and a headache. These symptoms would prompt her to take a blood pressure reading and it would always be elevated. The doctor began belittling her story, saying people don't take blood pressure readings at three a.m. and that "You don't take blood pressure as a hobby." He went on to ask about her level of education and diet, inquiring as to whether she ate a lot of canned soups, bologna, and other preserved meats. Always careful of her diet, Mom was offended not by the question, but by the suggestion of negligence and by his tone.

After this session my mother was shaking. On the way out I spoke with a nurse about the doctor's attitude and decided to escalate the complaint to the administrative level, contacting patient relations. A representative there half-heartedly took notes and indicated she would try to schedule Mom to see someone else in the future.

But that wasn't good enough. Eventually I wrote a detailed letter of complaint which resulted in Mom receiving a formal apology for her experience.

As Mom's advocate I was there for a reason, and I didn't like the helpless feeling of being ignored—unable to provide important details about her medical issues when she wasn't fully capable of speaking for herself. As her advocate I made a conscious effort to respect Mom's position as the patient. I tried not to intervene if she was slow to answer or had a moment of frustration or uncertainty. But I didn't want her to give inaccurate information, and I didn't want an attending physician to go away with a false assumption about her condition based on understated or omitted facts.

Early on I learned that medical professionals sometimes have unreasonable expectations about the amount of information patients and family members have readily at hand. As my mother's advocate I have disciplined myself to keep detailed records including dates and approximate times of her vitals, symptoms, and physical complaints, along with their frequency, her weight, medications, and other basic data.

Mom was being treated by a number of providers— among them a primary care doctor, an endocrinologist, and a cardiologist—who changed her medications frequently, looking for the right combination to stabilize her blood pressure and other vitals. She was whipsawed by this constantly changing chemical brew and its varying, sometimes alarming side effects. Although Mom might be aware that things didn't feel right, she was often at a loss to describe just what was wrong. The drug cocktail began to slow her heart rate to the point that a pacemaker had to be implanted. Attempting to monitor and interpret the effects of heavy medication can be tricky, especially for family members with little understanding of drug interactions and who lack other training and preparation for administering medicines. Those who are given to dismissing unidentified symptoms as just another sign of old age could be ignoring life threatening side effects.

As a first line of defense, family caretakers are the closest patient observers. Their daily, hands-on contact with the patient can help bridge the yawning gap between initial treatment and follow-up medical visits— a gap where emergencies and patient declines often occur. In my caregiving role I felt fortunate to have extensive personal medical experience, training as a paralegal, and an inclination toward independent research to support my self-education. Each proved to be a great resource. The thing that I could have benefitted from most—training specifically geared to me as a family caregiver—was nowhere to be found.

Big changes are now taking place in the medical field. Efforts to achieve universal health insurance coverage, dramatically cut costs, and speed the introduction of new technologies are changing health care culture. Our traditional, paternalistic model of health care delivery encouraged the perception of doctors as sources of unquestioned ability who operated as autonomous and authoritative decision makers. This perception was reinforced through decades of television shows and other forms of mass messaging that depicted doctors as miracle-working superheroes.

People are now being asked to erase this deeply embedded image, replacing it with a cooperative concept that urges patients, their advocates, and their families to be equal participants with physicians in maintaining health and wellness. But as with most top-down, policy-driven changes, hospitals, clinics, and other health delivery institutions can change much faster than norms and expectations that have become well established in the general population. Also patients, their advocates, and families are being actively encouraged to ask questions and voice their opinions about health care matters at a time when the entire health care industry is transforming and ever more complicated. That represents a subtle but massive shift of responsibility for health care outcomes. Patients are now expected to be co-authors of their health care narratives. Yet the vast majority has been conditioned to put their trust and their fates entirely in the hands of the physician and the traditional health care establishment. As a health care consumer, patient advocate, and family caregiver, I see a huge disconnect here, a widening gap between expectations and capacity on both sides of the patient/physician relationship.

In countless brochures, newsletters, bulletins, and other literature distributed by hospitals and clinics, I read the brightly worded messages urging patient activism. The problem is that most of this messaging originates within the facility. From the point of view of both patient and family caregiver, a visit to a hospital or clinic is usually under some form of duress. Someone is ill, or receiving follow-up treatment/observation for an ongoing or recent illness, and worried and stressed about the reason for being there. From the standpoint of mental preparedness, this is not the best environment for distributing guidance and instructions. Even if a person takes the literature home, it is unlikely to be studied right away, as other matters related to household and life usually intervene. As described in an earlier example regarding literature distributed at caregiving conferences, once the typical caregiver is able to relax in a moment that supports careful reading and retention of such information, fatigue and exhaustion usually take over. They lack both the energy and mental bandwidth needed to absorb that information. Distributing this information may meet a formal obligation of the hospital or clinic; however, in reality the publications act more like disclaimers than effective education.

Especially poignant are the directives to patients that they write down questions they want their doctors to answer, that they find an advocate, that they keep a list of their doctors and the medications prescribed, and so forth and so on. For the sixty-five and over crowd, growing by approximately ten thousand persons every month, these directives may be confusing, or just not make sense. This is precisely the age group that has been most completely conditioned to accept the physician's absolute authority. *Why does a person need an advocate when being seen by the doctor?* Many are enfeebled in some way—poor eyesight makes reading difficult, failing memories, attention and comprehension compromised by multiple medications, etc. If family caregivers—providers of the overwhelming amount of home-based care to people over fifty in our country— are to respond to such directives on the elderly patient's behalf, they deserve effective training and support in discharging those duties. The protocols and procedures of our new, emergent, health care delivery system require a higher level of engagement by both caregiver and patient. These are some things to consider:

- Speak up about terms you may not understand, like "hospitalist."
- Take notes in treatment situations. Record the names of doctors, nursing staff, and technicians, what is discussed with them, and requests/actions they make of you as the patient's advocate.
- Keep a current list of all medications taken, including over-the counter drugs and supplements, plus list allergies and other relevant health information. Include proof of insurance, Medicare, Medicaid, or other payment guarantees. Also include contact information for the care recipient's primary physician. Store it where it can be quickly accessed in case of an emergency.

- Inquire about important issues such as discharge policies, observation status, payment arrangements, and referrals for follow-up assistance at the *beginning* of the hospital admission/treatment process.
- Search out opportunities for caregiver education (workshops, conferences) and training.
- Remember, as primary caregiver, you are the "subject matter expert" with regard to the care recipient's overall health condition and care plan. Feel, act, and be empowered.

CHAPTER 10
Not the Least of Things

Everything that has been touched on so far in this conversation is of great importance to the family caregiver and those on the receiving end of that care. From dealing with the unique circumstances that lead to each instance of caregiving, to working through family relationships and drawing up critical legal documents, the front end of caregiving is loaded with gut wrenching emotions and hard decision making. Then there is the actual work of providing care, dealing with doctors, hospitals, and other health providers, as well as administering medications, monitoring for adverse drug symptoms and watching for indications of decline. For the more than fifty percent of us who work, there is the task of balancing caregiving responsibilities with the imperative to earn a living. Then all too often there comes a time when it is plain—for whatever reason—that caregiving needs can no longer be met at home. Thus begins the process of identifying, screening, and qualifying for admission to a suitable assisted care facility. The choices range from relatively low cost personal care homes that offer basic aid and attendance to higher-end establishments proclaiming luxury and comfort, to full-time nursing care. If beds are available, it is all a matter of what the care receiver and her family can afford.

But there is another category of adjustments that can be easily overlooked until one finds oneself in a caregiving situation. Those changes apply to the home, its layout, features, and manner of organization. Whether the care recipient lives in the caregiver's home or care is provided at the care recipient's home, most of these issues are relevant. The first set of challenges relates to physical design. Unless one lives in a recently developed fifty-five and older retirement community, it is unlikely that a home has been designed specifically to accommodate people with physical limitations imposed by aging.

My home, a 1200 square foot one-story bungalow seemed adequate as long as my mom was able to move about independently, had good motor functions and reasonable dexterity. Even then, especially because she was on medicines that could cause dizziness and temporary lapses of awareness, I was careful to remove obvious obstacles and eliminate trip/fall hazards such as throw rugs and magazine racks. As she aged, Mom experienced greater disability from surgeries and osteoarthritis, and movement came to require external physical support in the form of a walker. The use of a walker and eventually, the addition of special toileting equipment exposed the inadequacy of my bathrooms. They were far too small to accommodate a disabled person and her necessary equipment. The bedroom doors were narrow—as was the hall—and carpeted, creating drag that required extra effort when pushing the walker. Getting in and out of the bathtub was an ordeal that made me wish many times for a walk-in shower. There were inadequate handholds and pull bars in the baths, and really, no place to install them.

As difficult as it sometimes was, Mom was able to maneuver around the house fairly well and safely, mainly because the house footprint was compact and everything was located on one level. Had I lived in a two-level dwelling, she would have been confined to just one floor since going up and down stairs unassisted was pretty much out of the question. The huge numbers of baby boomers entering old age, at a time of increasing concern about the cost of institutionalized care, suggests that many of them will be aging at home. I would speculate that most of the houses they or their family members inhabit are not adequately designed and equipped to accommodate adults enfeebled by seven, eight, or nine decades of living. Retrofitting of homes is an option for some, but renovations are expensive, a cost many will not be able to afford. Renovations and additions made to accommodate a disabled person are also tricky and full of construction-related hazards. While the inside of my house was tight for my disabled mother's use, ingress and egress became downright dangerous. The house sat on a raised foundation so that going into and out of both exterior doors required navigating steps. Eventually I had no choice but to consider adding a wheelchair ramp onto one of the porches.

When Mom arrived at my house I had no reason to visualize a time in the future when she might be disabled to the point that I would need to build a handicapped ramp onto my house. Therefore I never looked at my house, its positioning on the lot, and physical relationship to my neighbors' properties, with thoughts of building a handicapped ramp in mind. When the time came that I needed to build that ramp, all those factors came very much into play. As it turned out, handicapped ramps, like other improvements, are governed by building codes. My front porch was so close to my property line that there was not enough land to allow the ramp to descend at its required grade from high point to low. The only option was the side/rear porch. The edge of the side porch was just a few feet from my property line, and the lot was irregular, slanting inward as it ran from the street toward the backyard, meaning the ramp would have to be squeezed onto a small sliver of land available between my house and the neighbor's property. It happened that the width of that strip just allowed the ramp to be built to code. There was so little room to spare that the corner of the ramp sits hard against a property survey stake. And that doesn't even address the cost of the project, nor the problems and issues with the tradesmen hired to do the job. Luckily I am a homeowner and had the option of making this improvement. Had I been a renter my only recourse would have been to put Mom in assisted living years earlier, or move. This is just one example of the kinds of problems that can spring up out of nowhere, an example of the unexpected hazards built into the caregiving enterprise.

According to the Centers for Disease Control each year 2.5 million older people are injured in falls. About twenty percent of falls result in serious injuries such as broken bones or head trauma resulting in 700,000 people being hospitalized at a cost of $34 billion. As Mom got older, especially in her eighties, a combination of things put her at high risk of falling: physical weakness and pain from joint problems; heavy doses of medication; failing vision; and increasing difficulty with movement and balance. The greatest risk of falling, other than tripping over obstacles, appeared to arise from situations where she had to exert herself in performing simple tasks that required reaching or extending to a point where her balance was lost. To reduce the risk from this kind of accident, I began to reorganize the household, placing frequently used items in places convenient to her—meaning within easy arm's reach. The goal was to eliminate her need to stretch or lean, both of which threatened balance. Placing kitchen items, medications, cosmetics, small appliances, and other household goods at or near waist level also eliminated the temptation to stand on raised surfaces to reach items overhead, or bend over or squat to reach items stored low. For ordinary items that could not be placed in this way, we kept a couple of "grabbers," spring-loaded poles with rubber tips that could be used to grasp distant objects without straining. Reorganizing household items in this manner was not a complicated undertaking but required constant, mindful attention to the placement of everyday things, a caution more or less automatic with young children but often overlooked with aged adults.

The caregiving literature is teeming with accounts of people who care for others so intently they end up neglecting themselves. As professionals take note of caregiver exhaustion, distraction, bloodshot, dark circled eyes, and flowing tears, they usually offer that worn phrase about caregivers' need for emotional support, counseling, and sympathetic encouragement. I offer this:

- *Throughout the home*: To accommodate an elderly, disabled adult a general reorganization may be in order. Move frequently used items (such as food, plates, tableware, toiletries, clothing, appliances and controls such as TV remotes) to levels and areas that can be accessed without straining. Remove throw rugs and easily tipped over furnishings; add bathtub mats and grab bars. Install railings on both sides of stairs. Make sure the home has adequate lighting. Use brighter light bulbs. One out of three people over the age of sixty-five falls each year, but less than half tell their doctor. Falling once doubles the chances of falling again according to the Centers for Disease Control. One out of five falls causes a serious injury such as broken bones or a head injury. A modified toilet may be needed or merely convenient. Check door widths to ensure wheelchairs or walkers can pass easily.

- *Access:* Some homes will require installation of a handicapped access ramp for wheelchairs. Check local building codes and homeowner associations for possible guidelines and requirements.

- *Bedroom:* Watch out for hanging bed linen.

- *Hydration:* Offer water frequently. Dehydration—loss of fluid and electrolytes—is a common problem among older adults for many reasons including decreased thirst, prescription medication, and illness. Total body water content of a person over the age of seventy-five is about fifty percent less than a younger person. Don't be dismissive of confusion and weakness; it might not be "just" dementia. Extra diligence in monitoring for dehydration is a wise practice.

- *Special tools:* The reacher/grabber reduces the need to bend over while standing or stooping. It also reduces the temptation to stand on objects to reach items stored overhead, which can result in loss of balance and serious injury from falls.

- *Dressing:* Purchase clothing and shoes that fasten with Velcro or comparable materials. Avoid laces, small zippers, and snaps.

- *Medication management:* Use an app for your smartphone like AARP Rx, vibrating pocket pillbox, or a programmable medication reminder and organizer.

CHAPTER 11
Epilogue

My mother passed away on April 20, 2016, just six weeks before her ninety-first birthday. It was a quiet, peaceful passing, so fleeting that sitting right there at her bedside, I could not say exactly when it happened. This was the end that I hoped for, that I had worked to achieve—one that was calm, dignified, and without needless discomfort. My work as a caregiver to Mom was over. What remained was the planning of final rites and wrapping up her worldly affairs. Despite the great burden of loss and despair in the wake of losing her, the legal arrangements we had put in place made executing those tasks far easier than they might otherwise have been. I was deeply grateful for the care we had taken in preparing for these inevitable events. Although the process had sometimes been uncomfortable and frustrating, the outcome was worth it—a smooth, relatively trouble-free transition.

Mom's passing was also a time for reflection. Our twenty-five years together had slipped by so quickly. At age sixty-three, I was now nearly at the age she was when we agreed that she would come to live with me. That realization caused me to think about my own approaching decline and on a larger scale, the mass decline of this large generation of which I am a part. My mom's generation was small but also strongly rooted in the traditional culture of our society, habits, and folkways mostly taken from a simpler, more rural and agricultural way of life. Families were not just intact, they were broadly extended. Bonds were strong and there were many reliable hands to call on for help in times of need. Today families seem more scattered, kinship ties weakened. The demands of family caregiving: time, resources, patience, sacrifice, and even hardship, are among the strongest tests of commitment. It probably isn't realistic to think that eroded values of collective strength and mutual support will be quickly regained. As my generation ages into its antiquity, there will probably have to be a great deal of creativity and innovation introduced to the care of older, dependent adults. Isolated individuals cannot bear this burden alone. A huge reckoning is at hand. National policies, administrative processes, and community priorities will all have to change.

My caregiving experience was, despite all its stress and toil, remarkably successful. For one thing I managed to remain employed throughout the 25-year period. Even with a progressive, flexible employer and adequate salary, I could not come close to covering the costs associated with late stage elder care services. North Carolina, where I live, is one of the lower cost states when it comes to home health care and assisted living services. According to an Annual Cost of Care Survey published by Genworth Financial, a leading provider of private long-term care insurance, the median *monthly* cost of a home health care aide in North Carolina during 2016 was $3,432. That works out to an annual cost of over $41,000. The annual median household *income* for North Carolina in 2014, according to the U.S. census, was only $46,556. In other words, it would take nearly the entire household income of the typical North Carolina family to afford a few hours of commercially provided home health care each month for a disabled adult.

Other costs are similarly unaffordable. Genworth calculated that adult daycare services in North Carolina have a median cost of $1,078 per month. Assisted living arrangements weighed in at $3,000 per month. Private rooms in nursing homes were $7,452 per month but semi-private set ups could be had for the relative bargain of $6,570 per month. And once again, according to Genworth, an acknowledged authority on this subject, North Carolina is one of the lower cost states. In fact, some of North Carolina's services have experienced recent price *declines*. It goes without saying that for the average family such costs are not sustainable. Even with fairly substantial retirement savings (which most people do not have), individuals and families attempting to pay for these services out of pocket would quickly run out of money.

Medicare, the national medical health system for people over sixty-five, does not pay for long-term care services—the kind that seventy percent of Americans who reach age sixty-five will eventually need. Eligibility for Medicaid, which does pay for long-term care, is determined by strict limits on income and assets. To qualify for Medicaid, individuals have to "spend down" their wealth until they reach a level of impoverishment that qualifies them for financial assistance. (The financial "look back" period that determines eligibility runs five years and involves producing bank records over that period.) My mom had no assets and a very low fixed income. Nevertheless she was deemed to be not qualified for regular Medicaid coverage. Her monthly income was just fifty dollars over the limit. Once she became severely disabled however (and after a long, tortuous process), I was able to secure support for Medicaid long-term care assistance that allowed me to put her in a nursing home. All of these benefit systems are random in design. Medicare, Medicaid, private long-term care insurance, and the Veterans Administration all have their own rules and procedures. There are endless forms to fill out, delays, and runarounds. Although an individual might qualify for multiple sources of support, as my mom eventually did, the systems are not aligned, each resource having a separate start-up and unique process, as though each time she was presented for benefits, a different person was applying. The effect is redundant, brutal, and heartbreaking for a caregiver.

According to the report of the Congressional Commission on Long-Term Care, "Medicaid is the single largest payer for paid long-term services and supports (LTSS). Today, Medicaid pays for 62 percent of paid LTSS, while more than 22 percent is paid out-of-pocket, and other private payers pay for only 12 percent." The "other private payers" are mainly insurance companies. The economic value of unpaid family-based caregiving, $234 billion as calculated by the Congressional Budget Office and referenced earlier, dwarfs all these sources. So why is unpaid family-based caregiving so invisible, so unappreciated, and so neglected? In large measure that is due to the way family caregiving is conducted: "on the down-low." It is for the most part a hidden, almost secretive activity that nearly everyone, especially those giving the care, is reluctant to speak about. When I would have conversations about caregiving with others doing the work, we would almost invariably shift to a muted tone of voice. After a while I began to ask myself, "Why are we whispering?" It's as though there is a stigma attached to caregiving as something shameful or embarrassing. In fact caregiving is generous and brave, even heroic. It is nothing to be ashamed of.

In order for unpaid, family-based caregiving to come out of the shadows, for it to receive the recognition, the appreciation, and accolades it deserves, caregivers will have to start valuing themselves and their work. They will have to begin to comprehend the objective, measurable, economic impact they have on communities and to the nation in the same way they understand the humanitarian gifts they bestow on those receiving care. Caregivers will have to demand more enlightened policies with regard to family leave and workplace practices, as well as better training for the home-based medical and therapeutic care they provide by default. They want and deserve more respectful treatment by doctors, hospitals, and the medical establishment. But family caregivers will also have to do some changing of their own. They will need to outgrow a habitual impulse toward secrecy and isolation by recognizing that that they are not alone. At any given time there are well over thirty million adults providing support to older people in America. That is a massive number, a movement. As our society continues to age rapidly in coming years, improving and expanding this huge unpaid resource will be of vital importance to everyone.

In other words the legions of silent, suffering, unpaid family caregivers will have to come out of hiding and into the light. Surrender some secrets. Become more visible, more vocal, more demanding, more expert, and more capable. If they do, a great many burdens will be lifted as society recognizes their contributions and responds accordingly. Caregivers don't need more well-meaning but fast dissipating sympathy. They need useful knowledge, thoughtful training, and the right tools for doing their jobs. That is the way forward. If it is taken, caregivers, those they care for, our communities, and the nation will benefit immensely.

SOURCES

Hafner, Katie. "As Population Ages, Where Are the Geriatricians?"
http://www.nytimes.com/2016/01/26/health/where-are-the-geriatricians.html

The National Alliance for Caregiving (NAC) and the AARP Public Policy Institute. *Caregiving In The U.S. 2015.*
http://www.aarp.org/content/dam/aarp/ppi/2015/caregiving-in-the-united-states-2015-report-revised.pdf

Commission on Long-Term Care *Report To Congress*, September 30, 2013.
https://www.gpo.gov/fdsys/pkg/GPO-LTCCOMMISSION/pdf/GPO-LTCCOMMISSION.pdf

Span, Paula. "Even Fewer Geriatricians in Training". January 9, 2013
http://newoldage.blogs.nytimes.com/2013/01/09/even-fewer-geriatricians-in-training/

Genworth Financial, Inc. *Genworth 2015 Cost of Care Survey.*
https://www.genworth.com/dam/Americas/US/PDFs/Consumer/corporate/130568_040115_gnw.pdf

Centers for Disease Control and Prevention. "Important Facts About Falls" http://www.cdc.gov/homeandrecreationalsafety/falls/adultfalls.html

Chamberlin, Jamie. American Psychological Association. "Little Known Caregivers"
http://www.apa.org/monitor/2010/10/children.aspx

Shell, Elizabeth. PBS Newshour. "The $234 Billion Job That Goes Unpaid"
http://www.pbs.org/newshour/rundown/the-234-billion-job-that-goes-unpaid/

RESOURCES FOR THE READER

National Hospice & Palliative Care Organization
Advanced Care Planning
http://www.caringinfo.org/i4a/pages/index.cfm?pageid=3277
http://www.caringinfo.org/i4a/pages/index.cfm?pageid=3289

Next Steps In Care Family Caregiver Guides
http://www.nextstepincare.org/Caregiver_Home/

ACKNOWLEDGEMENTS

Some books are more difficult to write than others. This one was very difficult. It forced me to dredge up many uncomfortable memories that I would rather have left buried beneath the deep layers of past experience. The Caregiver's Secrets forced me to think hard and critically about what I thought to be a uniquely personal journey only to discover that in the larger context of our aging society, this journey wasn't just my own, but one shared by 34 million other people more or less like myself. That was both a revelation and a source of motivation.

To my beloved daughter, Equia, thank you for patience beyond measure, for never encouraging the occasional drift into wishful thinking. You fill my heart to bursting. There were many times when I was close to abandoning the project, only to be rescued by your steady encouragement and wise counsel. You accompanied me on much of this journey, sharing a household with your grandmother and me from middle school until departing for college. With your knowledge of long term care issues, you were invaluable as a sounding board, a filter, and a source of calming reassurance. As a writer, you vastly improved the readability of the narrative.

A special nod goes to my "buddy," who provided meals and assistance with deferred maintenance on my abode while cultivating a beautiful garden outside my window; who cajoled me into resting when I'd forgotten the definition of enough, and said no with such an effective cadence. I am grateful for your friendship.

To my brothers, Wilbert and Maurice, because "none goes *her* way alone."

My gratitude goes to those who have been like sisters: Deborah, Margie, Ann, Anita, Marion, Ethelyn, Rhonda, Barbara, and Vanessa. To the professionals who helped me to understand: Belinda Rochelle, Juanita Nelson and Karen Segovia.

Professor Nancy M.P. King (not related, but much admired) of the Wake Forest Institute for Regenerative Medicine, Wake Forest Medical School, and Co-Director of Wake Forest University's Center for Bioethics, Health & Society, read an early draft of the manuscript and became a major champion. Her critical comments on the text and precise suggestions for improvement made this a much more accurate and useful book. Some wonderful friends and supporters—several of them experienced caregivers—also served as readers and offered valuable input. Many thanks to Priscilla Barbee, Bill Kelley, Anna Hembrick, Scott Jackson-Ricketts, Rich Robeson, and all the Willinghams (Alex, Kwame, and Lumumba) for their time, effort, and helpful remarks.

And, a final thanks to the NC Writers Network.

ABOUT THE AUTHOR

A native of Spring Lake, North Carolina, Willetha King Barnette earned a Bachelor of Arts from North Carolina Central University, and paralegal certification through Duke University. She has worked in educational environments for more than thirty-five years, including an international insurance industry trade association, in university settings, and small private institutions. She has served as a volunteer guardian ad litem in the juvenile court system, a hospice volunteer, and a patient advocate for cancer victims. She is active in health advocacy causes including organizations dedicated to curing breast cancer and Crohn's disease, as well as efforts to improve caregiving for the elderly and disabled. She resides in Durham, N.C.

Made in the USA
Columbia, SC
30 January 2018